ONCE UPON A TIME

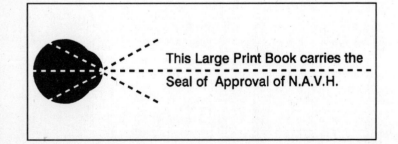

ONCE UPON A TIME

DISCOVERING OUR
FOREVER AFTER STORY

DEBBIE MACOMBER

THORNDIKE PRESS
A part of Gale, Cengage Learning

GALE
CENGAGE Learning·

Detroit • New York • San Francisco • New Haven, Conn • Waterville, Maine • London

GALE
CENGAGE Learning·

Library of Congress CIP DATA on file. Cataloguing in publication for this book is available from the Library of Congress
ISBN-13: 978-1-4104-5900-8 (hardcover)
ISBN-10: 1-4104-5900-4 (hardcover)

Published in 2013 by arrangement with Howard Books, a division of Simon & Schuster, Inc.

Printed in the United States of America
1 2 3 4 5 6 7 17 16 15 14 13

*to Lois Dyer fellow author and
special God-given friend*

CONTENTS

Dear Friends,
Did you hear the one about. . . .

Oh my goodness, you won't believe what happened to me . . .

Once upon a time a . . .

When we hear those words, we pause and listen because we know we're about to hear a story. Everyone loves a story. What do you remember about the last sermon you heard? My guess is a story the preacher told to illustrate his point. That was exactly what Jesus did. He told stories, stories so rich they have touched lives every generation since.

Because I am primarily a fiction writer, one question I ask myself as I plot my books is "What if?" My mind starts playing with the idea of plot twists and unexpected turns taking the reader on a journey that all started with a "what if" question.

The point of this book is that we are writing our own stories, the story of our lives and we are sure to encounter plenty of twists and turns along this pathway called life. My hope is that these seventeen chapters will resonate with you as I tell my own story and hold open the door for you to consider yours.

As an author I work with an incredible publishing team. I would be remiss if I didn't credit those who have worked so hard to craft this idea into a book . . . a story for you, my reader. First and foremost my agent and dear friend, Wendy Lawton. Wendy is amazing. Organized, articulate, talented, and generous. This is my first book working with editor Beth Adams, and I hope it's one of many. Rebekah Nesbitt, editor in chief of Howard Books is a bright shining star in the publishing arena. Anyone who has the pleasure to work with her sings her praises, and I'm happy to join that choir. Publisher Jonathan Merkh is amazing. He saw the vision for my nonfiction titles and has been a constant friend and encourager. I love you all and thank God for the opportunity to work with you.

Debbie Macomber

You can reach me in a variety of ways: my website at DebbieMacomber.com or on Facebook or by writing me directly at P.O. Box 1458, Port Orchard, WA 98366.

ONE:
IN THE BEGINNING . . .

Let the redeemed of the Lord
tell their story.
— PSALM 107:2

Once upon a time, in a land not far away, I grew up dreaming of castles, handsome knights, and princes on fiery steeds, like many young girls. My family was an ordinary one, with a mother and a father and one wicked brother who sold copies of my diary to all the boys in my junior high class.

Every fortnight of my childhood I would journey to the library, seeking more tales of valor and knights. As I opened the heavy library door, juggling a stack of books, the hush of the cavernous room felt like a medieval priory. The smell of books and ink, leather and floor wax, brought a smile of eager anticipation. Usually I had finished my last book the night before and couldn't wait to begin a new adventure, hopefully one with knights willing to carry me off to the land of enchantment.

Because I am a slow reader, it took me a long time to read each story. Consequently I relished every scene, each fair maiden and fearsome dragon. I never understood why other kids were able to read so quickly. Not me. I had to read each sentence slowly and thoughtfully, but word by word, the story emerged. Like magic. I'd venture to faraway places, reading about princes and castles, but I also read about girls who lived in small towns just like Yakima, Washington.

After returning my stack of books to the counter, I would head for my favorite corner of the library to begin the deliciously difficult job of choosing a new stack of books. As I slid a book off the shelf and fingered the adhesive label on the spine, I anticipated the adventure I knew was tucked between the covers.

Someday . . . perhaps I could write these kinds of stories. Already the ideas whirled around inside my head. I never could read a book without making up a story of my own.

That dream never changed. I knew I wanted to write stories someday. Stories that would sit on library shelves just like these. Stories just waiting for someone to open the cover and join in the adventure.

Most people smiled indulgently when I shared my dream. Once, when I told a teacher that I planned to be a writer and one day I would write a book, she smiled and patted my hand. "You can't write, Debbie," she said. "Why, you can't even spell."

But the dream refused to go away.

Then one day, when I was only nineteen, a handsome electrician drove up in a shiny black convertible. It wasn't a steed, but I knew a prince when I saw one, and before long we were married. Soon we were living in a two-bedroom cottage with a white picket fence.

As often happens when a fair damsel meets her Prince Charming, children followed, and soon the two-bedroom cottage became a four-bedroom castle. The kingdom flourished and prospered, and between soccer games and car pools, ballet classes and clarinet lessons, I dreamed about love and enchantment and the magic of romance. Money was scarce in those days, but there was never a shortage of books. Our four children knew their mommy loved to tell stories. That was a good thing, since they loved to listen to them. As I fixed frugal feasts that could stretch a pound of hamburger six ways to Sunday, I still dreamed

15

of writing books and telling stories.

A dream that never dies eventually demands attention. Despite a budget that allowed nothing frivolous, I took that leap of faith and answered the call to write. We rented a typewriter for twenty-five dollars a month. Twenty-five whole dollars! That was a big chunk out of the castle coffers in those days.

But I faithfully wrote on that typewriter every day. I spun stories, wrote articles, and kept at it faithfully, despite receiving rejection after rejection. After a number of years, my patient prince came to me with a handful of bills. "Darling," he said as he put his arm around me, "I'm going to have to ask you to get a job. Something that pays money."

I looked at my typewriter, sitting on the kitchen table beside a mountain of typed pages tied into book-sized bundles with twine.

"We're just not making it," he said, "and I don't know what else to do."

I knew he was right. Maybe the fairy tale was ending. I knew that I couldn't work, care for the kids, and still follow my dream. Maybe some dreams were just not meant to come true. I packed away the manuscripts and cleaned up the typewriter in preparation for returning it.

That night I didn't sleep. I kept thinking about my dream.

In the wee hours, the prince stirred and saw me awake. "What's wrong?" he asked.

"I think I could have made it," I whispered. "I don't know why, but I think I could have made it as a writer."

My prince was quiet for a very long time before he took my hand. "If it means that much to you, then go for it." He squeezed my hand. "We'll figure something out. We'll do whatever we have to do so you can write."

And somehow we got by. Every day the two older children came home from school to the sound of typewriter keys clacking away. My big break didn't happen the next year. Or the next. In fact, it didn't happen for five long years. Then one day I received that magical telephone call. A publisher offered to buy my book.

That special story was the first of a whole bookcase full of books I would eventually write. I wrote book after book, and, I am grateful to say, readers bought those books. Some even went to the very library I used to haunt as a child. With confidence, they slid my books off the shelf, knowing they would find satisfying stories tucked between the covers.

To this day I walk up the staircase into my writing turret and continue to tell stories. Even though my publishers have sold more than one hundred million of my books, I am not finished telling stories.

I plan to write happily ever after.

I was born to be a storyteller. I've read stories, collected stories, written stories, and loved stories my entire life. There are no words that stir my soul more than "once upon a time."

I relish every aspect of being a writer, but through the years I've had an insight about myself as an author: I'm happiest when I'm writing. Don't get me wrong, I enjoy meeting my readers, doing interviews, and everything else that is involved in my career, but in the end — and the beginning — I am a writer, and telling a story is what's most important to me.

The very first time I visited that library in my hometown, I was only four years old. When Miss Bunn, the librarian, handed me that very first book — a Little Golden Book — my mother said I took it with both hands, looked at it for the longest time, and then pressed it against my heart. My mother could not pry the book away from me. My love of books never waned. I struggled with reading until I was ten years old, but once the concept of sounding out words took hold in my mind, those books I carried home from the library never gathered dust. I read them under the covers long after the lights should have been out. I knew I needed to sleep, but the story kept moving forward, and I was caught up in the magic and wonder of it all. This was the same magic and wonder I longed to create some-day myself. When I finally closed the book, sleep still eluded me. I would often lie awake into the wee hours of the morning, reliving the plot and the beauty of the story . . . and dreaming of one day creating my own.

I began to fantasize about writing my own stories not long after those library days. It didn't matter that I suffered from what I came to understand was dyslexia or that I was a creative speller. (I still am!) I knew I wanted to tell stories. A fellow writer, Katherine Anne Porter, said it best: "A story is like something you wind out of yourself. Like a spider, it is a web you weave, and you love your story like a child."

What I didn't know at that time was that not only would all my writing wishes come true (above and beyond anything I could have ever dreamed or imagined), but I would come to see my own life as one grand story.

That's what this book is about. Not the stories I write, nor the story of my life, though both will be part of the telling. I wanted to write this book to talk about Story. Story with a capital *S.* I want to help you view your own life as one continuous story. One never-ending story. And when you do, I hope you will recognize how God has held you in the palm of His hand the same way He has me.

Madeleine L'Engle, in her book *The Rock That Is Higher: Story as Truth,* wrote:

Story makes us more alive, more human, more courageous, more loving. Why does anybody tell a story? It does indeed have something to do with faith, faith that the universe has meaning, that our little human lives are not irrelevant, that what we choose or say or do matters, matters cosmically. It is we humans who either help bring about, or hinder the coming of the kingdom. . . . Our truest response to the irrationality of the world is to paint or sing or write, for only in such response do we find truth.[1]

We are the stories other people read. Those stories have power — power to heal and power to change, power to direct and encourage. Story enriches our life and the lives of those around us.

As I travel around the country and talk to people, I see stories. One of my joys when meeting readers is hearing their stories. Often they touch and inspire me, and again I am reminded that God has been able to use even me, through the power of story.

WHAT IS STORY?

People have told stories as far back as we can trace. I recently listened to a recording of my friend Liz Curtis Higgs speaking about the story of Ruth from the Bible. Ruth lived about 3,200 years ago, but the book of Ruth wasn't committed to writing until the ninth century BC. That means that the story was preserved in oral tradition from generation to generation. Those who don't understand the sacred trust of an ancient storyteller might wonder how faithful the story eventually recorded was to the actual event. No worry. There's little chance of change. Generations heard these stories over and over and the tiniest deviation would be cause for the storyteller to be run out of the village ahead of an angry mob.

21

People take their stories seriously.

Each culture has had its storytellers, from the Scottish bards to the African griots. Storytelling has been a noble profession from earliest memory. Eventually stories moved from oral tradition, the spoken word, to the written word. With the advent of the printing press, these marvelous tales of old migrated to books. In modern times, our stories are also told on screens both large and small.

E. M. Forster, in his classic book *Aspects of the Novel,* likens story to a tapeworm, its beginning and end completely arbitrary. He illustrates his point with the storytelling of Scheherazade, the legendary Persian queen and narrator of *One Thousand and One Nights,* summing up the fact that the story is about, in three simple words, *what happens next.* Here's what Forster wrote:

Scheherazade avoided her fate because she knew how to wield the weapon of suspense — the only literary tool that has any effect upon tyrants and savages. Great novelist though she was — exquisite in her descriptions, tolerant in her judgments, ingenious in her incidents, advanced in her morality, vivid in her delineations of character, expert in her knowledge of three Oriental capitals — it was yet on none of these gifts that she relied when trying to save her life from her intolerable husband. They were but incidental. She only survived because she managed to keep the king wondering what would happen next. Each time she saw the sun rising she stopped in the middle of a sentence, and left him gaping. "At this moment Scheherazade saw the morning appearing and, discreet, was silent." This uninteresting little phrase is the backbone of the *One Thousand and One Nights,* the tapeworm by which they are tied together and the life of a most accomplished princess was preserved.[2]

Aren't we just like Scheherazade's husband, in that we want to know what happens next?

WHY TELL STORIES?

Storytelling is a natural, time-honored way of making sense of seemingly random events. When I am writing my books I'll often begin by telling several different stories that seem unconnected until, little by little, I bring the stories and the characters together and start to intertwine them. By the time the reader reaches the end of the book, hopefully the plot has magically come together. I explain, when people ask, that this form of storytelling is like braiding hair. Each thick strand is turned over the others, building, one upon another, until the braid is complete.

Culminating all the elements of the plot is important. We work to make sense of the world around us. We want to make sense of the people we know and of what is happening to us. The writer Joan Didion said, "Had I been blessed with even limited access to my own mind, there would have been no reason to write. I write entirely to find out what I am thinking, what I am looking at, what it means."

THE GOD WHO TOLD STORIES

From the time I was that little girl with a dream, I also had a hunger for God. I didn't really come to know Him in the same close relationship I enjoy now until after I was married and had two of my children. Still, for as long as I can remember I had an unquenchable longing for Him. From the moment I intentionally made Him the centerpiece of my life in 1972, I've taken the book He wrote and read it faithfully cover to cover each and every year. And you know what I realized? The Bible, from the first pages of Genesis, has plenty of lessons and ideas, proverbs and poems. However, when Jesus came along, He was the God who told stories. Moses may have delivered the tablets that began with "Thou shalt not . . ." but Jesus sat down with an expectant crowd gathered around Him and began, "A farmer went out to sow his seed . . ."

So we will look at story through the pages of this book. You'll notice that I've pulled familiar phrases from classic stories and folktales for the chapter titles. For me, just hearing the words "a long, long time ago," or "in a faraway land," or "happily ever after," offers a sense of anticipation, of excitement and expectation. A story is about to unfold, and those key words tell all we need to know about the kind of story it will be.

Liz Curtis Higgs, in talking about the story of Ruth, tells us that the Hebrew word that opens the story, *wayehi,* which is translated as "In the days," or "And it came to pass," actually embodied so much more to those Hebrew listeners. When they heard *wayehi,* they leaned in eagerly so as not to miss a word, because it literally meant, "Trouble is on the horizon but redemption is coming."

Don't you love that? With a single word,

the author of Ruth managed to capture the attention of the audience. Now that's the power of a good storyteller.

YOUR OWN GRAND STORY

I've come to realize that God wants us to see our lives in terms of story — from an eternal perspective. Trouble is on the horizon — it's always there in one form or another — but we have nothing to fear because redemption is on the way. Or, as you've seen written on T-shirts, "Please be patient, God is not finished with me yet."

As we explore ways to see our lives as one grand story, we're going to realize that all the parts — the good parts and the bad, the trouble and the heartache, the disappointments and the discouragements we face — are important to the story, and, as we already know, redemption is coming!

GATHERING THE STORY TOGETHER

Remember the scene in the movie *Out of Africa* where Karen Blixen's native major-domo, Kamante, inquires about the stack of manuscript pages she has on her worktable? She tells him it is her book. He points to the manuscript. "This is not a book." Kamante goes to the bookshelf and takes out a book. "This is a book," he says patiently.

He turns the book upside down. "See, this pages don't fall out." He puts his hand on the stack of loose pages and asks how she will make "this pages" into a book.

He is asking an age-old question, really. What do we do with our story, with all these stories we are gathering? I'll have to admit, I'm a little uncomfortable bringing up the subject of journals. Someone pointed out once that I have talked about journals and journaling in every single one of the nonfiction books I've written. I can't help myself. I'm a writer. A storyteller. If we are going to collect stories, we need to have some way to keep them and to pass them on. We can't rely on our memories. Those are too fleeting. I am so grateful for the journals I've written through the years. They are my legacy to my children, my day-to-day ramblings about my life, my dreams, my hopes, and my happenings.

If we are going to live intentionally — if we are going to pay attention — we need to capture ideas and stories in some way. The easiest way is, of course, journals. Just get a blank book or even a writing tablet. Aside from the diary I kept as a child, my earliest journal, when our family was young, was a spiral-bound notebook. It was all we could afford. Your own need not be fancy. What's important is that you begin to write down everything you remember and collect. For the last few years I've used my journal sort of like a collection tool — a scrapbook — for letters or special birthday cards, announcements, or newspaper articles. You can organize your journal any way you like. Develop your own system, but, in the meantime, just begin to capture the everyday details of your life and write them down.

I have the journal my mother kept during World War II while my father was overseas. It was one of those five-year ones, with only a few lines for each day. It amazes me how much my mother was able to say with a few short sentences. Mom and Dad were married just before my father shipped overseas. Two days after the wedding ceremony my father was on a troop carrier taking him to England. One of my favorite entries is from the day Dad had roses delivered to Mom for their anniversary. I'm certain he involved his youngest sister, my aunt Gerty, in this. The entry in Mom's diary says: *Roses from Ted. Oh, my heart.*

Six simple words that say so much.

Madeleine L'Engle called her journal a "commonplace book." It was a big brown Mexican leather notebook. She copied words that caught her fancy, passages from books, quotes, and sayings. She said, "All I'm looking for in it is meaning, meaning which will help me live life lovingly."[3]

You might not be a paper-and-ink sort of person. You may be more comfortable creating a journal on your computer. There are many apps and software programs available for this very purpose.

Like Madeleine L'Engle, I also write down quotes and sayings that attract my attention. I keep those in my Gratitude Journal. (Yes, I keep more than one journal. What can I say? It's the writer in me.)

Something else from Madeleine L'Engle — she said, "When I have a profound personal experience, I write it down in my journal and that way I am working through it. To some extent, I am objectifying it. It is no longer just subjective. But I'm also setting it in my memory. If you want to put it in a novel or a book, it does have to wait. It's very important to set down what you're feeling while it's happening."[4]

The important thing is to write it down. Don't worry about "doing it right" or about grammar or about writing a memoir that will hit the *New York Times* best-seller list. Just get the descriptions and stories down in your own words.

Trust your voice.
Trust your stories.

HOW TO USE THIS BOOK

In writing this book, I'm not suggesting everyone needs to pen his or her own memoir or record his or her story for posterity. This is more about developing an awareness — a commitment to remembering. That's not to say I'm not going to encourage you to record your story in some way for your family or begin a journal or two. But I am going to look at the elements that make up a good story and ask you to think about the story God is writing with your life. One of my favorite quotes is from Socrates: "The unexamined life is not worth living." Look at your own life and my guess is that as you do, you will see God's fingerprints, His loving, guiding hand upon you.

So let's dig in and start figuring out ways to examine our lives and tell our stories. Here are some ways you may want to explore your own story:

- **Telling your story in a group setting.** After you read through this book, you may want to gather a group of friends or a women's group at church or your reading club and go through the book together. I offer what I call storytelling prompts at the end of each chapter to help tickle your memories and offer something to chew on. These prompts make great conversation starters if you use this book in a group setting. (After all, there is nothing better for getting to know people than sharing stories.)

- **Telling your story through journaling.** You might want to take a journal and use the storytelling prompts to begin to explore your own "once upon a time." But don't stop there. As I talk about story, apply my story and the stories of others in the book to your own life. What was your beginning? Who are the characters in your story? What unique challenges have you had to face? If you allow yourself to write freely, you'll be surprised at the things you remember.

- **Telling your story through the arts.** Some readers are not writers. Writing in a journal sounds like a school assignment to them. That's okay. You might want to tell your story through the pages of a photo album or scrapbook. If so, get out your scissors and glue and begin to piece your own story together. If you are a quilter, there is a great tradition of storytelling quilts, like album quilts. We can be creative in how we tell our stories.

- **Telling your story out loud.** Folktales and fairy stories all started out in the oral tradition — told around a fire. You may want to revive this storytelling tradition in your family. When we tell stories about ourselves to our families we forge the strongest link possible — shared history. I think it would be great fun to use the storytelling prompts at the end of each chapter as dinnertime conversation starters. If a child is allowed to tell his own story at the table, he will begin to see his life from a broader perspective. And, of course, it is important to let each story be told without correction or interruption. (We'll talk more about quieting the critics later in the book.) Just think of the richness that awaits us if the table or the gathering holds many generations that can share stories together. Don't forget, we pass along our values, generation to generation, through storytelling.
- **Telling your story through memoir.** If you are interested in writing your

own memoir, go for it! You'll be leaving a treasure for your family.

Shall we start?
Once upon a time . . .

Storytelling Prompt
What is your "In the beginning" story as told to you by family? What is your own earliest memory?

The Importance of Remembering

Charles Lutwidge Dodgson, better known as the author who wrote *Alice's Adventures in Wonderland* under the pen name Lewis Carroll, knew the importance of remembering. He was a pioneer photographer who spent hours staging artful images of the people in his life. He kept journals and wrote books — both math books and his delightful Alice stories for children. But one of the ways he marked his life was to designate never-to-be-forgotten days as "white stone days." In his journals, he told about a particularly meaningful outing and then wrote, "Mark this day with a white stone." To him this meant that he knew he would pass that way only once and he wanted to remember.

Mark Batterson, the pastor of National Community Church in Washington DC, says in his book *Soulprint,* "Without memory, we'd have to relearn everything every day. Without memory, we'd forget who we are and where we've been. Without memory, we'd lose faith because we'd forget the faithfulness of God."[5]

Later in the book he says, "If you're willing to do some personal archaeology, you'll dig up some invaluable artifacts." And he goes on to say, "Digging into your past can be emotionally exhausting, but remember, your destiny is hidden there. Pray for a spirit of revelation. Make sure you have a journal to record your thoughts. Start looking for those mysterious symbols that can be turned into lifesymbols."[6]

Deuteronomy 4:9 says, "Only be careful, and watch yourselves closely so that you do not forget the things your eyes have seen or let them fade from your heart as long as you live. Teach them to your children and to their children after them."

Two:
In a Land Far Away . . .

Where can I go from your Spirit?
Where can I flee from your presence?
If I go up to the heavens, you are there;
if I make my bed in the depths, you are
there. If I rise on the wings of the dawn,
if I settle on the far side of the sea, even
there your hand will guide me; your right
hand will hold me fast.
— PSALM 139:7–10

When we open a book and read the words,
"In a land far, far away . . ." we fasten our
imaginary seat belts, because we know we're
going to find ourselves exploring a new
world between the covers of the book. That
line alone is capable of setting my heart to
racing with eager anticipation.

The setting of a book plays an important
part in story. I believe that setting is a
character in and of itself. If you've read
Daphne du Maurier's *Rebecca,* you'll never

forget that opening line, "Last night I dreamt I went to Manderley again." Manderley was as much a character — a mysterious, haunting character — as Rebecca or Maxim de Winter. The same goes for Emily Brontë's *Wuthering Heights*.

Several years ago, I sat down to work out details for a new series of books I wanted to set in a small town that gave my readers a sense of coming home — a sense that they could live in this town and feel like a part of the community. The advice often given to writers is to write what you know. Over the course of my career, I'd written a number of books set in series. The first took place in Alaska, the second in Texas, and yet another in North Dakota, creating towns and populating them with characters my readers might well find in their own communities. However, before I wrote a single word, I visited each of those locations and read countless books so I had the flavor and the feel of the area. As my career moved forward, I found I was often on the road. It was time for a new series, and so I decided to create the fictional town of Cedar Cove, a thinly disguised version of my own hometown of Port Orchard, Washington, on the Kitsap Peninsula. I say thinly disguised because Cedar Cove has a library with a mural that bears a striking resemblance to Port Orchard's library and mural. Imagine that! And the Pancake Palace looks an awful lot like Port Orchard's own Family Pancake House. In fact, Cedar Cove's famous D.D.'s on the Cove is reminiscent of the real Amy's on the Bay, on the Port Orchard waterfront. And in Port Orchard there's a marina, a park with a gazebo, and a totem pole, just like in the book. In fact, so much of Cedar Cove resembles Port Orchard that I published a map for the Chamber of Commerce to hand out to the hundreds of tourists who routinely stop by for a tour of our town. As the books gained popularity, readers came to Port Orchard to visit Amy's on the Bay and the Family Pancake House and the other sites they had come to know from the books.

Remember what I said earlier about the success of my career going above and beyond anything I could have dreamed? That has certainly been the case with my Cedar Cove series. Who would have imagined when I decided to set my new series in Port Orchard that the town would one day become a tourist destination? Certainly not I.

As you can probably tell, I had fun creating this semifictional town. In all, I wrote twelve novels, plus two Christmas books and a novella, as part of the Cedar Cove series. Cedar Cove became known as "the town you'd love to call home."

As tourists started coming into town, the Chamber of Commerce took notice, and so did the town leaders and the city council. A group of business leaders and politicians came to me and suggested we stage an event — that we "open up the town" for readers. A committee formed, and in August of 2009 a five-day celebration dubbed Cedar Cove Days took place, with readers coming from forty-two states and seven foreign countries, all to celebrate a fictional town in a land far away.

Readers love the Cedar Cove series. They love the feeling that comes over them when they reach for the next installment, because they know they are going to meet characters they have come to love in a location that makes them feel as if they are stepping out their own front door.

My readers often asked me how many books would be in the series, and my response was always the same: I'll stop when all the stories are told. When I felt I had reached that point, I came up with a new, exciting concept and announced the last book of Cedar Cove series, tying up all the loose ends and revisiting each family one last time.

Oh my, I have to tell you, the outcry, the response to ending this set of stories — it took me completely by surprise. My mailbag began to swell. Readers weren't ready to leave Cedar Cove. They seemed to be mourning the loss of the places and characters that were familiar — that had become a part of their lives. I remember receiving a letter from one of my readers when Olivia, the town judge, was diagnosed with breast cancer. The reader said she had started to pray for Olivia before she remembered Olivia was a fictional character.

I wondered if they were so upset because at some point in our lives so many of us moved away from our families and hometowns — our roots — to follow jobs or spouses' jobs. Maybe it was because we yearn for that town where we know all the people and they know us. Possibly it was just because we hate to come to the end of a story.

Well, I've always listened to my readers. More than once, they have changed the course of my career. I wasn't about to ignore them on this point. By the time you read this, the first book in my new series, *The Inn at Rose Harbor,* will have been published, and I've plotted the second. And where did I decide to set this wonderful inn? The bed-and-breakfast that is the centerpiece of the Rose Harbor series is set right in the middle of Cedar Cove. (And the Inn at Rose Harbor somehow looks an awful lot like Port Orchard's Cedar Cove Inn.)

LONGING FOR A PLACE

There's something we discover about ourselves in the places we come to love, even if they are places from fiction or from our own imaginations. C. S. Lewis, in his book *Surprised by Joy,* described how a longing for place — for a setting — was an early clue to his nature. Here he's talking about one of the first glimpses of that longing for something he couldn't yet describe:

This absence of beauty, now that I come to think of it, is characteristic of our childhood. Once in those very early days my brother brought into the nursery the lid of a biscuit tin, which he had covered with moss and garnished with twigs and flowers so as to make it a toy garden or a toy forest. That was the first beauty I ever knew. What the real garden had failed to do, the toy garden did. It made me aware of nature — not, indeed, as a storehouse

40

of forms and colors but as something cool, dewy, fresh, exuberant. I do not think the impression was very important at the moment, but it soon became important in memory. As long as I live my imagination of Paradise will retain something of my brother's toy garden.[1]

And a little further along in the book, he reprises that memory, that little garden:

The first is itself the memory of a memory. As I stood beside a flowering currant bush on a summer day there suddenly arose in me without warning, and as if from a depth not of years but of centuries, the memory of that earlier morning at the Old House when my brother had brought his toy garden into the nursery. It is difficult to find words strong enough for the sensation which came over me.[2]

When C. S. Lewis wrote *The Lion, the Witch and the Wardrobe,* that toy garden, that longing for something he couldn't describe, became the land of Narnia — a setting that has touched the imaginations of children ever since.

Sometimes our longing for a certain place — or, as in Lewis's case, a longing for a deep, otherworldly beauty — is a clue God gives us about who we are and what we are called to do.

REVISITING HOME

Many classic settings have become legendary — some fictional, some real. How about *Anne of Green Gables*'s Prince Edward Island? Garrison Keillor's Lake Wobegon? Scarlett O'Hara's Tara? When I say Narnia or Middle Earth, doesn't it conjure up a picture? How about Pemberley? Or *The Secret Garden*?

Or what about our own settings? In the first chapter I talked about Yakima and the library I loved in my hometown. A big part of who I am today was shaped by my hometown.

Every year I host what we call Grandma Camp. It's a time I set aside to spend with my granddaughters doing something fun and different and new. Last summer my three granddaughters and I held Grandma Camp in Yakima, Washington, the town where I was born and raised, where I lived the first seventeen years of my life. I showed them the hospital where I was born (it has a new name now) and the house where I grew up (new owners, of course). The house where Mom and Dad lived when I was born burned to the ground in the late 1950s. We visited the church where my husband and I were married (the priest who married us has since left the priesthood). We also stopped where my high school once stood (St. Joseph Academy, now, sadly, is a parking lot). I showed them the building where my father made and reupholstered furniture. It really brought home how much time changes everything.

Previous Grandma Camps have included traveling to exciting locations like New York City, where I introduced my granddaughters to my love of theater. It was a big step down, from New York City to Yakima. I was worried the girls would be bored by my small-town memories. I needn't have been concerned. They did me proud. They were fascinated by my childhood and wanted to know how we did things "in the old days." They asked me countless questions about my youth, about my friends, about my school days. By showing them my own history, reliving my own childhood, I shared with them the very things that shaped me into the woman I became. My hope is that one day they will look at their lives differently and will learn that they too are shaped by their life experiences, by their friends, their schools, their own history.

When I look back on my childhood settings, I can see God's hand so clearly over my life. I can see the seeds of who I became from those earliest days. The English writer Graham Greene said it best: "There is always one moment in childhood when the door opens and lets the future in."[3]

For me, those moments came during my childhood in Yakima. A good example of this was when my eighth-grade teachers held a fashion show with all the sweaters and items I had knit. Because I'm dyslexic, school was always difficult for me, and Sister Seraphina looked for a way to show me that while I struggled with reading, math, and just about every other subject, I had the ability to create something beautiful. I could be a success. So she organized the show to showcase the things I had knit. This came at a time when I badly needed a sense of self-esteem, an identity. I became known as the knitter. Who knew what a profound effect my love of knitting would have on my life . . . and my writing career?

Another example of the importance of setting in shaping my life is the hours I spent at my father's upholstery shop. The feeling I had in my father's shop crept into my writing. In my novel *A Good Yarn,* I wrote, "The flower boxes immediately reminded me of

44

my father's first bicycle shop, and it was almost as if my dad was giving my venture his nod of approval. The colorful but dusty striped awning sealed the deal in my mind. I knew this old-fashioned little shop could become the welcoming place I'd envisioned — and it has." My father did not have a bicycle shop, but I was describing the feeling of a daughter whose father was proud of her choices. That came straight out of my own life.

Anne Rivers Siddons, when asked about the Southern settings of her books, described those settings like this: "When you get into the smaller towns, the suburbs, you see everything through a kind of shimmer. . . . It's like all those years, people and events dance a little 'squim' in front of your eyes and you see everything through that."[4]

Don't you love that? All the years, all the people . . .

As we begin to remember our own stories, it's important to consider our own settings. The home of our childhood. The neighborhood or city streets. Our church. Our school. Our friends. Our extended family. As we reexplore our roots, it becomes easier for us to identify those seeds of who we are today. For instance, that fashion show that Sister Seraphina arranged for me may well have sparked my lifelong love of knitting and birthed the novels that have centered around knitting. Or my father's upholstery shop — which forever colored my attitude toward small businesses — may have been the impetus for the creation of Blossom Street, a community of small businesses created as a setting for the series of books by the same name.

Take out your photographs and look at them with new eyes. Like the clues and glimpses C. S. Lewis discovered as he reached back into his childhood to the memory of that tin box his brother had decorated. When you do, you'll discover that God has already planted those seeds deep within you and you should be able to trace their germination.

HUMBLE BEGINNINGS

Writer John Updike offered this advice in *The Writer's Digest Handbook of Short Story Writing, Volume II*:

No soul or locale is too humble to be the site of entertaining and instructive fiction. Indeed, all other things being equal, the rich and glamorous are less fertile ground than the poor and plain, and the dusty corners of the world more interesting than its glittering, already sufficiently publicized centers.[5]

Updike was talking about interesting settings for fiction, but don't you think those humble, dusty settings make some of the best settings for growing interesting people as well?

I've met people who seem embarrassed about their humble beginnings. Don't be. Think of Jesus. He chose to be born in a stable. We've heard those words — born in a stable — so often we no longer imagine it with our senses. We picture the artistic crèche of Christmas that is lovingly familiar, with angels at hand and shepherds kneeling reverently before the manger.

When was the last time you visited a stable? Do you remember an actual barn being anything like that? Unless it had just been mucked out and scrubbed down, Jesus's birthplace would have been less like an exquisitely sculpted Fontanini nativity scene and more likely to make the Holy Family gag. Yet out of that rank stable came the Savior of the world.

When we consider the setting God chose for His only Son's arrival into the world, doesn't it make us want to think about the settings He chose for us?

Describe the house of your childhood — the one you remember best. Take us on a tour, pointing out the quirky things and the parts that make you wish you could go there again. Be sure to include ethnic details, the good, the bad, the scary, and all the things that make your roots unique.

Recognizing the Seed

Even when I was a young child, the clues about who I would become were all there — my love of books, knitting, storytelling, cooking, swimming, family, Christmas, and all things spiritual. God planted the seeds of my lifelong pursuits before I even had language to express the desires.

I don't think that is unusual. Recently I read about William Morris — writer, decorative artist, and designer. He is considered to be the single most influential designer of the nineteenth century, leading the Arts and Crafts movement. His designs and patterns were inspired by nature, with a distinctive medieval influence. It shouldn't have been a surprise to anyone who knew him as a child. At four years old, he was already reading Sir Walter Scott. The boy loved all things medieval.

He even wore an authentic, child-sized suit of armor when riding his pony into Epping Forest. His biographers point to his childhood fascination with forests, gardens, flowers, and birds — all seeds of the art he would later produce.

Watch the children around you. When you observe a child absorbed in a particular interest, chances are that interest will only deepen with age.

As you begin to delve into your own story, take special note of the origins of your adult interests and longings. I'm guessing you'll find the early signs of your grown-up interests and passions in things you loved as a child. "It is like a mustard seed, which a man took and planted in his garden. It grew and became a tree, and the birds perched in its branches" (Luke 13:19).

THREE:
IN THE DAYS . . .

Remember the days of old;
consider the generations long past.
Ask your father and he will tell you,
your elders, and they will explain to you.
— DEUTERONOMY 32:7

When we think about telling our stories, we tend to think in terms of events. What came next? Many writers do the same — we call it plotting out the story. Equally important, however, is discovering what came before. That's referred to as backstory. It's the important history of what happened before page one that motivates the hero or heroine for what is about to happen, for what comes next. In other words, the backstory is what leads up to the story that's about to unfold. It's everything that went on to get the characters to the place they are, mentally, physically, emotionally, and spiritually, when the story opens. By the time I write the opening line of a new book, I know each character's motivation, because I know his or her history. You may never see the back-story, but if I didn't have it, the characters wouldn't ring true. A good writer knows that if you added all of the backstory into a book, it would end up being a thousand pages — too much backstory slows down the action. We've all read books in which the writer dumps tons of information that has nothing to do with the story itself into the narrative. Those are usually the books we end up putting down after reading only a few chapters. The book has gotten bogged down in detail and the author has lost sight of what's important to the reader. And what's important to the reader is the core story. But you can't get there if the author doesn't know the backstory.

The author creates the backstory in order to get the story right. J. R. R. Tolkien was the master of backstory. He created his Middle Earth world rich with legends and lore. He spent so much time on it that some of his backstory eventually became novels in themselves, like *The Silmarillion*.

THE STORY IN CONTEXT

As you think about telling your own story, one of the first things you need to consider is your own backstory. We've heard it said hundreds of different ways: we are products of our age — children of a particular place in history and our unique setting. Our environment shapes much of our thinking. For that reason we'll want to explore our backstory.

An important part of backstory is setting the milieu. Milieu is a French term that has no exact translation into English. It means the social context, circumstances, setting, time, and even the sphere in which the characters live and the action takes place. It's the ethos of a period, not just a chronicle of events. For instance, I grew up in the fifties and sixties. The milieu included the controversial birth of rock 'n' roll with Bill Haley and His Comets and the much-talked-about hip swivel of Elvis Presley. We enjoyed a carefree postwar optimism, the move to suburbs from the cities, and the idea that space might even become a new frontier with the launch of *Sputnik*. We saw a sharp rise in the fascination with the automobile and our national optimism was reflected in the soaring tailfins on the backs of cars. The advent of television changed the way we viewed ourselves, and we began to sense its influence on our lives. It was the age of hula hoops and hot dogs, processed food and French fries, drive-in movies and sock hops, boys in cars and . . . well, you get the picture.

My own milieu was unique, though it did include many of those iconic fifties elements. While the nation turned on black-and-white televisions to watch Donna Reed baking cookies and doing her housework in a freshly ironed cotton shirtwaist dress, apron, and high-heeled shoes, my own mother was a working mother. I didn't come home to freshly baked cookies and a Donna Reed–like mother who couldn't wait to find out how my day went. I came home to an empty house filled with books, an empty kitchen where I could cook, and a knitting project in my school bag. My milieu helped shape the person I became. And because of my hardworking parents — parents who loved my brother and me, even though their love didn't look like the television sitcom kind of love — I knew early on what it meant to juggle home and work. And my mother was every bit as stylish as Donna Reed.

My world consisted of Catholic school, complete with uniforms and nuns, and a whole passel of cousins who lived nearby, went to school with me, and became like brothers and sisters. Oh, what incredible fun we had together.

And my milieu included books that took me out of my world and landed me in all kinds of different places. Children who are readers become romantics in the classic sense of the word. They live far beyond their own scope.

CAPTURING THE DETAILS

Sometimes it is difficult to catch the ethos of the era — the sense of immediacy. One of the ways to do that is to focus on details. Reread some of the descriptions above, like the size of tailfins on cars — make note of those unconnected details that come to your mind when you read that. These sorts of details often come up when we are talking with siblings or longtime friends. Sometimes just one detail will evoke a flood of images. "Remember old Mrs. Miller? Remember how she used to go out to the sidewalk with a knife and peel the wax blobs off?" You could take your notebook and scribble in this memory, plus the details like "the sidewalks of our childhood had greasy spots of melted wax all around the corner store, the remains of wax lips, wax mustaches, pickles wrapped in wax." Those quirky details will usually spur further memories. If you are writing about these memories, or even talking about them around the table, you might want to explore how you reacted to those things. When you add your reaction, you've added another important layer to the storytelling fodder. Like: "When I looked at those blobs of wax on the streets I used to wish I lived near the pristine sidewalks of Mayberry." Or you might imagine what your mother would have said if she ever caught you spitting gum or wax on the sidewalk.

In her book *Bird by Bird: Some Instructions on Writing and Life,* Anne Lamott offered a favorite story starter: "Sometimes when a student calls and is mewling and puking about the hopelessness of trying to put words down on paper, I ask him or her to tell me about school lunches."

It seems that everybody has a school lunch story.

She goes on to tell her own lunch story. "Here is the main thing I know about public school lunches: it only looked like a bunch of kids eating lunch. It was really about opening our insides in front of everyone. Just like writing is. . . . The contents of your lunch said whether or not you and your family were Okay."[1]

Lamott advises her students to "start with your own story." She'd say, "Plug your nose

55

and jump in, and write down all your memories as truthfully as you can. Flannery O'Connor said that anyone who survived childhood has enough material to write for the rest of his or her life. Maybe your childhood was grim and horrible, but grim and horrible is Okay if it is well done. Don't worry about doing it well yet, though. Just start getting it down."[2]

Just as backstory does for a novel, these details will add texture and interest to your own story. Chances are, remembering them will offer even more clues about why you are the way you are.

DEEPENING THE STORY

In addition to the milieu of your life, you'll want to plumb the depths of your own backstory. Who were your people? Where did they come from? What is your spiritual legacy? My own family were Germans who had settled in Russia. They were hardworking farmers. I can trace much of my work ethic and love of family to my grandparents and their parents, who left Russia for a new life in America.

Many of you have rich immigrant stories in your family, too. That's your backstory. Delve into your own history and that of your grandparents and great-grandparents.

You might be amazed by what you find. There is something powerful in the stories of people who uproot themselves from everything and everyone they know and head into the unknown. We're going to talk a little bit about the hero's journey in chapter 7, but the immigrant story is a classic take on the hero's journey. If your people came to America by way of Ellis Island, for instance, make the trip there. Trace the names on the wall. Try to imagine the adventure.

I wonder how many of us can catch even a small whiff of the fear that must have been part of the immigrant experience. Can you imagine being in a strange culture where you can't communicate and probably have precious few resources? Like my maternal grandfather, many left their entire families behind, forsaking all that was familiar and comfortable. One of the most stirring things I saw when I visited Ellis Island was the strands of woven hair that immigrants brought with them — hair from those they loved and had left behind.

In every family that emigrated, there were a multitude of fears and dreams. Dig beyond the surface. Maybe Papa wanted to come. He longed for land, for a hope and a future. Mama, on the other hand, had to say goodbye to her own aging parents and to all her sisters who lived in the same village. She may have had to leave an oldest daughter behind because of a longstanding betrothal. They would miss the wedding. Who would prepare the wedding supper? Would there be grandchildren? Mama knew that in all likelihood she'd never see them again. Never hold them close to her heart.

Some immigrants embraced the adventure. Others hated to leave friends and familiar surroundings. A writer knows that it's not hard to tell the story of an avid adventurer who enthusiastically starts out on a journey. Think about it — where's the inner conflict in that? It's too easy, because he relishes the challenge and it costs him nothing to leave. But give us a painfully shy girl whose stomach gets knotted at the very thought of change . . . now, *there's* a story.

Once you begin to collect your own back-story, you'll have the raw material to tell many different stories in any number of formats. The important thing is to write it down. You'll be surprised to discover new meaning — richness you never intended or expected — as you go back later and reread what you've gathered.

Come up with ten quirky things from your growing-up days that modern kids wouldn't understand. Describe the one piece of clothing you wore as a child that you detested. Dig deeper: how did it make you feel?

Exploring Our Roots

Alex Haley, author of *Roots,* said this about discovering our story: "In all of us there is a hunger, marrow-deep, to know our heritage — to know who we are and where we have come from. Without this enriching knowledge, there is a hollow yearning. No matter what our attainments in life, there is still a vacuum, an emptiness, and the most disquieting loneliness."

One of the ways to dig into your background and discover your history is to become involved in genealogy. Learning to research family and discover your ancestors is far more than idle curiosity. Here are some of the reasons you may want to begin shaking the family tree:

- **Preserving interesting cultural traditions.** If, during your research, you find out that your family hailed from Scotland, say, it offers a whole new layer of interest to your heritage. Bring on that kilt!

- **Helping you reconnect with family, far and wide.** Enthusiasts cite this as one of the most enriching reasons to do genealogy. Many have connected with long-lost relatives who share the same interest in history.

- **Allowing you to explore your spiritual heritage.** Church records are a treasure trove of information. Finding artifacts like old family Bibles can bring you closer to knowing the spiritual legacy of your family.

- **Giving you a personal connection to history.** Memorizing dates and places in school never sparked a love of history like finding an ancestor who fought in the Civil War or settled in Jamestown Colony.

- **Uncovering important medical information.** There have been cases of people who were able to trace a genetic anomaly from nothing more than sleuthing through their genealogy.

- **Connecting to new places and new communities.** You may find yourself tromping around old graveyards or small-town libraries, but travel takes on a whole new excitement when it is a history treasure hunt as well.

- **Demonstrating the value you put on family.** As your children see you putting an emphasis on ancestors and family history, they come to understand their place and their responsibility in being part of a legacy.
- **Helping you connect with famous personages from history.** This is the fun part. As you dig around, you're likely to find a number of ancestors worthy of special mention (along with a few you will avoid mentioning at all).

FOUR:
THERE ONCE WAS A MAN . . .

For you created my inmost being;
you knit me together in my mother's
womb. I praise you because I am fearfully
and wonderfully made; your works are
wonderful, I know that full well.
— PSALM 139:13–14

What makes a book you will never forget? Is it a rollicking story line? Sometimes, but what do you think made us fall in love with *To Kill a Mockingbird*? It wasn't the story line, though that was excellent. It was the character of Atticus Finch. What about *Gone with the Wind*? Yes, it's a great Civil War novel, but it was Scarlett O'Hara and Rhett Butler we could never forget.

People often ask me where I get my ideas for the stories I write. Because my gift is storytelling, this aspect of being an author comes naturally to me. Story ideas are all around us; life itself presents us with plenty of material each and every day. It's a matter of being open to the stories happening around us and then fashioning them into a narrative with believable and compelling characters. It's not as much about ideas as it is about characters for me. And I think most writers find that the people around them provide the basis for the fictional characters they create. I certainly do. It can be a matter of taking a trait from one person, a physical characteristic from another, a way of speaking from someone else, and then combining all those distinguishing traits into one person. Ultimately, believable characters come from the writer's observations about the people and situations surrounding him or her.

CHARACTERS — FEARFULLY AND WONDERFULLY MADE

I chose Psalm 139:13–14 as the verse to open this chapter because it gives us insight into how God created characters — and by characters, I'm not talking about fictional characters; I'm talking about us. He knit us together (don't you love that?) in our mothers' wombs. He created our inmost beings — it's the ultimate backstory. We are fearfully and wonderfully made.

That's as humbling as it is profound. God

took my grandfather's brown eyes, my great-grandmother's thin brown hair, bits and pieces of ancestors I never knew, and created me.

I am never closer to my own Creator than as I create my story world and craft characters for my books. In my fiction, I am mimicking what He did in creation. I am awed by the work He did. As I came to the end of my Cedar Cove series, I found myself overwhelmed by the sheer number of characters, trying to keep everyone separate in my mind and all their stories and connections with the other characters straight. Yet look at the vast number of people God created. I'm speechless. No two of His "characters" are the same. We've always heard that and always believed it, but with many of the mysteries of DNA being decoded it has become even more astounding how each person is completely different. And not only is every "character" God creates unique, but He keeps track of each one, even as far as knowing the exact number of hairs on his or her head (Luke 12:7).

We are all main characters in a rich and complex story of our own.

And each character is fearfully and wonderfully made. Complex. Multifaceted. Unique.

Just as we explore characters in writing, I want us to consider the characters in our own stories. Later on, in chapter 10, we are going to look at secondary characters, but in this chapter we're talking about the main characters, mostly the protagonist. In your story, that protagonist is you.

THE UNLIKELY HERO

The small, plain Scottish woman with home-cropped hair and bushy eyebrows, wearing a dress that was long out of style (had it ever been in style in the first place?), walked out on the Clyde Auditorium stage for the television show *Britain's Got Talent*. No one knew it at the time, but she'd spent much of her life as a caregiver for her widowed mum, who'd died just two years before. She hadn't been able to sing since her mother died, but because her mum always wanted her to try out for the show, the painfully shy Susan Boyle swallowed her fear and auditioned.

As she stood alone in the center of the stage, looking for all the world like some-one's maiden aunt, the judges smirked and asked a couple of condescending questions. She replied clumsily and self-consciously. The cameras panned to the audience. Three thousand eyes rolled; some people whispered to neighbors, others laughed outright.

Susan Boyle was no stranger to ridicule. At birth she had been deprived of oxygen, which left her with lifelong learning difficulties. Kids teased her in school. Frizzy hair, slow learner, no sense of style, shy — it was all rich fodder for bullies.

One of the judges, Simon Cowell, asked what she was planning to sing. She answered with the title — "I Dreamed a Dream," the much-loved lament from the musical *Les Misérables.* The camera panned to the audience and there were outright guffaws. But when she sang the first line, mouths dropped open. By the third line the audience was on its feet, en masse, clapping wildly. Her voice was flawless. Even now it's hard to watch the performance without having tears stream down my face. The YouTube video of the event has been viewed almost one hundred million times. And if you're like me, you've watched it more than once, simply because it's breathtaking to watch the story of Susan Boyle and her talent unfold before the world.

Perhaps one of the reasons we love this story is because there's a bit of Susan Boyle in all of us. We may look small and inconsequential to the world, but we know that God has planted something big inside of us. In one way or another, we are all unlikely heroes.

CHARACTERS WHO COME ALIVE

Have you ever read a book in which you simply couldn't identify with the protagonist? Sometimes writers offer us an antihero, the nonheroic hero, but that main character must still retain some redeeming qualities or he or she won't resonate with the reader — and all too soon we set the book aside, never to reach for it again. Usually when we come across a character we don't like it's because the author didn't dig deep enough. We often call it a cardboard character. The outline is there, but the character is stiff and flat.

As a writer, my challenge is to create characters that become as real to my readers as their own neighbors. I give the characters dreams and challenges and then reveal how they react and grow when confronted with the challenges that bring them to the point where they can reach for their dreams. A good example of this is Lydia, the main character of *The Shop on Blossom Street*. Despite being a two-time cancer survivor with limited resources, she boldly opens a yarn store. It's her affirmation of life, her stand to declare that cancer will not rule her existence. It's an against-all-odds challenge for her, and that yarn store becomes the refuge — the gathering place — for the other characters whose stories are woven into the book. I can't tell you the number of readers who've written to me to ask me about Lydia. Her cancer survival story inspired some who told me they read the book while spending a long afternoon sitting at their oncologist's with an IV of chemo drugs dripping into their veins.

Some people have asked me if I have trouble writing from the male viewpoint. I've raised two sons and been married more years than I want to count. Living with men gives one a certain insight into the way a man thinks . . . or doesn't think. Seriously, it comes down to observation and honesty — which is true of all characters a writer creates.

Talking about characters who come alive, longtime editor Penelope J. Stokes wrote:

In all my years of editing, one experience stands out as the landmark example of a living, breathing character. I was working with B.J. Hoff on her *Emerald Ballad* series, dealing with the character of Finola — a beautiful young woman who, because of a traumatic event in her past, had not spoken since she was a child. "There's something wrong with Finola's character," B.J. told me one day on the telephone. "Something I don't understand. Pray that I'll find out what it is, will you?"

If that sounds a little odd, wait until you hear the rest of the story. I did pray, as promised. The next morning, I called B.J. and said, "I don't know if it's good news or bad, but I think Finola is pregnant."

A long silence ensued, and at last B.J. said quietly, "Yes, yes she is. And this baby is going to be the turning point of her spiritual life."[1]

This is how real our characters can become to us. As I'm writing my stories, I carry these people around with me, thinking about what they are doing and how they would react. They become as real to me as the real-life characters in my own story.

TELLING THE TRUTH ABOUT OUR CHARACTERS

The writer's challenge — your challenge as you tell your own story — is to make your characters come to life. Sometimes it's hard to see ourselves as others see us. It's even harder to see ourselves as God sees us. But as we tell the story and honestly chronicle the events, the characters begin to emerge. I think about *Little House in the Big Woods* and all the Laura Ingalls Wilder books. These books told the story of the Ingalls family's homesteading adventures in the late nineteenth century. The author intended these to be children's books, but over the years they have become classics, loved by adults as well as children. Her storytelling is simple and direct, but through her eyes we see all the characters growing, facing and meeting life's difficulties. They are complex, like Pa, who has little time for anything during the spring, summer, and fall, but come winter, brings his fiddle out while the family dances, sings, and tells stories, warmly tucked in against the frigid weather outside their log cabin. Through telling these stories of the way she views the world and interacts with her family and those around them, the main character, Laura, emerges.

Digging deep and trying to see ourselves as God sees us will help us flesh out our characters. I use the words "digging deep" as if it were an easy task, but it's one of the most difficult things writers do. In chapter 6 we'll talk about motivation, and depth comes partly from understanding what motivates us. In plumbing the depths of my characters, I ask questions. Why did that bother her so much? What is it he fears that raises the stakes? We need to ask the same kinds of questions about ourselves. Why does my stomach knot up every time someone raises his voice? Or, why do I fear this empty nest? Or maybe, why do I have such a hard time relating to a God who calls Himself my loving Father?

As we write or remember our stories, we need to keep asking the tough questions that will get us below the surface. The nice thing about digging deep is that it often challenges our long-held assumptions and beliefs. One friend recently wrote a novel that was loosely based on her own life. Her sense of worth had been shaped in part by the belief that her father didn't love her. But as she worked on the fictional father character in her book, she began to see things in her own father's life that explained, in part, his behavior toward her. The farther she got into the story of this fictional character, the deeper she got into her father's limitations. Eventually she began to recognize his clumsy attempts at showing his love. Fifty-some years later, it took a fictional character study to help her unlock a deeply troubling mistaken assumption.

As you explore your story, go deep, into your roots, your childhood, your friends. Don't skim the surface. It reminds me of the anecdote George Sayer told about leaving his very first meeting with his Oxford tutor, C. S. Lewis:

As I walked away from New Buildings, I found the man that Lewis had called "Tollers" sitting on one of the stone steps in front of the arcade.

"How did you get on," he asked.

"I think rather well. I think he will be a most interesting tutor to have."

"Interesting? Yes, he's certainly that," said the man, who I later learned was J. R. R. Tolkien. "You'll never get to the bottom of him."[2]

That's what I hope for as I write my own characters and work into the real characters in my own life — that I will never get to the bottom of them. Or, for that matter, the bottom of me.

Storytelling Prompt
Introduce a character or two from your childhood, describing them through the eyes of your child-self. Senses provide important character clues, so don't forget

to include visual details, smells, sounds, and other senses.

Why Listen to Your Life?

In his book *The Sacred Journey*, Frederick Buechner tells us why it is important to mine the depths of our lives:

What I propose to do now is to try listening to my life as a whole, or at least to certain key moments of the first half of my life thus far, for whatever of meaning, of holiness, of God, there may be in it to hear. My assumption is that the story of any one of us is in some measure the story of us all.

For the reader, I suppose, it is like looking through someone else's photograph album. What holds you, if nothing else, is the possibility that somewhere among all those shots of people you never knew and places you never saw, you may come across something or someone you recognize. In fact — far more curious things have happened — even in a stranger's album, there is always the possibility that as the pages flip by, on one of them you may even catch a glimpse of yourself. Even if both of those fail, there is still a third possibility which is perhaps the happiest of them all, and that is that once I have put away my album for good, you may in the privacy of the heart take out the album of your own life and search it for the people and places you have loved and learned from yourself, and for those moments in the past — many of them half forgotten — through which you glimpsed, however dimly and fleetingly, the sacredness of your own journey.[3]

FIVE:
AND HE WENT BY
THE NAME OF . . .

A good name is more
desirable than great riches;
to be esteemed is better than
silver or gold.
— PROVERBS 22:1 (NIV)

Names are important, both in storytelling
and in life. As I started to write *The Inn at
Rose Harbor,* the first book in my new
series, I determined to choose a meaningful
name for my main character. She was a
young widow. Her husband had died in
Afghanistan. She had come to Cedar Cove
in search of peace and a fresh start. I also
knew that the inn she purchased would be
the setting for many different guests who,
through the years, would come searching
for something significant. I knew this main
character, the innkeeper, would be part of
my life for a long time to come. She needed
the perfect name. I decided on Rose, but

not for her first name. Jo Marie Rose. Out of that surname came the name for the bed-and-breakfast — Rose Harbor Inn.

Rose is a name with great significance for me. My great-grandmother was named Rose, as was my mother. Our oldest daughter is Jody Rose and the granddaughter born on my birthday is Madeleine Rose. And the mother of my husband, Wayne, was Marie. Jo Marie Rose was the perfect name, one that I'll enjoy using for many books to come.

WHAT'S IN A NAME?

It might seem strange to spend so much time naming a fictional character, but names do more than just identify characters. We first sense this in reading about God assigning Adam the task of naming the animals. In Genesis 2:19–20 we're told, "Now the Lord God had formed out of the ground all the wild animals and all the birds in the sky. He brought them to the man to see what he would name them; and whatever the man called each living creature, that was its name. So the man gave names to all the livestock, the birds in the sky and all the wild animals." This is the Garden of Eden we are talking about — no busywork here. Naming had significance.

In John 10:3 we see that the Good Shepherd calls us by name. "The gatekeeper opens the gate for him, and the sheep listen to His voice. He calls his own sheep by name and leads them out." There's an intimacy in calling someone by name. Dale Carnegie said, "Remember that a person's name is to that person the sweetest and most important sound in any language."[1]

In a book I wrote many years ago I struggled with the hero's name and ended up changing it four times. He was a man who had been an outsider his entire life. He wasn't part of the "in" crowd in school. His mother had abandoned him and his father had little time for him, so he knew little of what it meant to be part of a family. He felt as if he skirted what life was supposed to be like. I finally settled on the name Cain. Cain because he was the first man born outside the gates of paradise. He was always on the outside looking in, just like my character.

We also see in the Bible that when a profound change happened in someone's life, they often had a name change to go with it. Abram became Abraham, Simon became Peter, Saul became Paul. It is interesting to see how names evolved. A few months ago, as I was reading in Genesis the story of Abraham's servant sent to find a wife for Isaac, I was struck by the use of the word *servant.* The story is told through the servant's eyes and the important part is his reaction to the miracle. Throughout the account, he is referred to as the servant or the senior servant, but after he prays and asks God for a sign, from that point forward my translation refers to him mostly as "the man." It's subtle, but it's the kind of name change, or descriptive change, that reminds me that prayer changes us. Our connection with God through prayer has a profound effect on us. Interesting.

In the book *Anne of Green Gables,* we learn much about the hopes and dreams of the imaginative orphan Anne Shirley when the practical Marilla simply asks Anne for her name.

"Will you please call me Cordelia?" she said eagerly.

"*Call* you Cordelia! Is that your name?"

"No-o-o, it's not exactly my name, but I would love to be called Cordelia. It's such a perfectly elegant name . . ."

"Unromantic fiddlesticks!" said the unsympathetic Marilla.[2]

And a little while later:

"Do you never imagine things different

78

from what they really are?" asked Anne wide-eyed.

"No."

"Oh!" Anne drew a long breath. "Oh, Miss — Marilla, how much you miss!"

"I don't believe in imagining things different from what they really are," retorted Marilla. "When the Lord puts us in certain circumstances He doesn't mean for us to imagine them away."[3]

I was like Anne and longed for a different name as a young girl. Most people assume my given name is Debbie, since it's the only name I ever use, but my mother, always the romantic, actually named me Debrae Lynn. The emphasis was on the last syllable, so to make it easier for folks to pronounce she had changed the spelling to DeBrae by the time I entered school. It doesn't matter, I've always been Debbie. My school already had a number of girls named Debbie, spelled all kinds of ways. I longed to be different. I thought Millicent was a beautiful name. Or Gretchen. In fact, I had an entire list of names. But alas, like Anne, I'm just Debbie, and you know what? I've grown rather accustomed to being me.

In my own family, names have always been important. Besides Jody Rose, I had Jenny

Adele, named after Wayne's mother, Marie Adele. A few years back, Jenny decided she was simply not a Jenny. The name didn't fit, so she chose to use her middle name, Adele. It's taken some getting used to and I think she'll always be Jenny in my heart, but I want to honor her decision and I do try to use Adele.

A Name Offers Insight into a Person's Character

People who study names and the impact a name has on an individual point to several important effects of a name. One is perception. A name tells us something about a person. If someone were to name a boy, say, Percival, no one would expect him to become a star in the wrestling world. The same goes for book characters. Louisa May Alcott, the author of *Little Women,* named her main character Josephine March, but had her go by the name Jo. It's fitting that she was a tomboy with a name like that. Even the name March — for a father who was a soldier and for Jo, who had drive uncommon in women of her day — was a perfect action name.

The age-old question that continues to be debated is whether a name influences who we will become or the person naming somehow senses — through genetics or family traits perhaps — who we will become. In other words, is a name a self-fulfilling prophecy or a true prophecy? No one's been able to answer that.

There is an obscure story in the Bible about a man named Jabez. At least, it was obscure until Dr. Bruce Wilkinson pulled two verses out of a whole long genealogical string of the descendants of Judah and wrote a little book, *The Prayer of Jabez: Breaking Through to the Blessed Life,* about being extravagantly blessed, based on the recorded prayer of Jabez. Here are those two verses: "Now Jabez was more honorable than his brothers, and his mother called his name Jabez, saying, 'Because I bore *him* in pain.' And Jabez called on the God of Israel saying, 'Oh, that You would bless me indeed, and enlarge my territory, that Your hand would be with me, and that You would keep *me* from evil, that I may not cause pain!' So God granted him what he requested" (1 Chron. 4:9–10 NKJV).

It is interesting that Jabez's name meant "pain." Doesn't that seem a cruel thing for a mother to do, to name her child for the pain he gave her? Jabez must have grown up always being aware of the meaning of his name, because when he prayed his bold

81

prayer, he asked God to keep him from evil so that he would not inflict pain. He overcame the meaning of his name. Now, all these years later, his name is associated with abundance and expanding territory.

The philosopher Maurice Merleau-Ponty wrote, "As has often been said, for the child the thing is not known until it is named, the name is the essence of the thing and resides in it on the same footing as its colour and form."[4]

Some believe a person's name or a character's name limits him. Merleau-Ponty also said that when one is named, it's like saying, "You are this; you are not that." He gives as an example the name Madeleine — my granddaughter's name. He points out that she will forever be associated with the teacups and madeleines of Proust, gastronomy, the queue of French schoolgirls from Ludwig Bemelmans's picture book *Madeline,* French culture in general, and all connotations that are carried with it.

It's an interesting theory, isn't it?

THE NAME AS A CHALLENGE

Remember the Johnny Cash song "A Boy Named Sue"? Originally a poem written by Shel Silverstein, the ballad tells the tale of a young man's quest for revenge on a father who abandoned him when he was three years old. If that wasn't bad enough, he stuck his son with the name Sue — a girl's name. Sue suffers bullying and mockery throughout his childhood, and because of it he grows up tough and mean. His mission in life is to find and kill his father for giving him "that awful name."

When he finally catches up with his father, he confronts him: "My name is Sue!" After formally greeting him, Sue announces that his father should prepare to die. They fight until they are both spent. As he finally catches his breath, Sue's father claims he named the boy as an act of love. Because he knew he would not be there for his son, he said, he gave him the name to make sure that he grew up strong. Learning this, Sue forgives his father. Not that he comes to terms with the name — Sue closes the song with a promise to name his son "Bill or George, anything but Sue!"

The song is tongue-in-cheek, of course, but it does illustrate that some names offer challenges. It's like being named after an iconic individual. You wonder what kind of effect that has on the recipient of that name. Did George Washington Carver distinguish himself in part because of the responsibility of his name? How about Martin Luther

THE MEANING OF A NAME

Most parents pore over baby-name books the whole time they are anticipating their child's birth. They work to choose a name that sounds pleasing and has a meaningful connotation. Most of us treasure our name stories. We all know people who were named for places like Virginia, Savannah, or Dallas. Others were named after family members, and still others for treasured objects, like Ruby, Daisy, Sterling, or Brandy. However we came by them, most of us are fascinated by the historic meanings of our names.

My own first name refers to the bee. Just simply the honeybee. When I think of the legendary diligence of the bee, I'm honored by that meaning. Hard work is important to me. Plus, the Bible has much to say about honey. It denotes richness. It usually refers to fullness of God's provision, like a land flowing with milk and honey. My maiden name, Adler, means "dweller at the sign of the eagle." I like that. Isaiah 40:31 is a favorite verse of mine: "But those who hope in the Lord will renew their strength. They will soar on wings like eagles; they will run and not grow weary, they will walk and not be faint."

And Macomber? Well, it simply means "son of Tom." Nothing profound there, but overall, can you see how intriguing it is to delve into the meanings behind your name? Knowing that names have great significance to God, it is worth the time it takes to explore our own names.

Go beyond the simple meaning in baby-name books. If your parents are alive, ask them what went into choosing your name. Find out about others who share your name. It's very easy to find out what names were popular when you were born. Were you given the "in" name for your milieu? If you were given an unusual name, did it give you permission to be unique? If you were named after a great personage, that says something about your parents' hopes and dreams for you. If your name appears in the Bible, what meaning is attached to it?

Dig deep. It's all part of your story.

Storytelling Prompt
Write about your name — what it means, why it was chosen for you, and how you feel about it. If you were to rename yourself today, what name would you choose? Why?

Just as coming to understand the meaning of your name and the effect it has had on your life is important, choosing a life verse helps you find a touchstone for your life. If I've ever signed a book for you, you'll notice that under my name I always write "2 Tim. 1:7." Many years ago I ran across that verse, which says, "For God has not given us a spirit of timidity, but of power, love and discipline." This became my life verse — whenever I feel afraid, or doubtful, or unsure of something, I repeat this verse to myself. I have whispered the words so many times they are part of me.

Search through the Bible to find a verse that has special meaning for you. To get you started in your search, here are a handful of possibilities that have inspired many.

- Jeremiah 29:11 (NIV): " 'For I know the plans I have for you,' declares the Lord, 'plans to prosper you and not to harm you, plans to give you hope and a future.' "
- Psalm 34:8 (NIV): "Taste and see that the LORD is good; blessed is the man who takes refuge in him."

- Isaiah 40:31 (KJV): "But they that wait upon the LORD shall renew their strength; they shall mount up with wings as eagles; they shall run, and not be weary; and they shall walk, and not faint."
- Mark 12:30 (NIV): "Love the Lord your God with all your heart and with all your soul and with all your mind and with all your strength."
- Romans 8:28 (NLT): "And we know that God causes everything to work together for the good of those who love God and are called according to his purpose for them."
- Romans 8:31 (NLT): "If God is for us, who can ever be against us?"
- Romans 8:38–39 (NLT): "And I am convinced that nothing can ever separate us from God's love. Neither death nor life, neither angels nor demons, neither our fears for today nor our worries about tomorrow — not even the powers of hell can separate us from God's love. No power in the sky above or in the earth below — indeed, nothing in all creation will ever be able to separate us from the love of God that is revealed in Christ Jesus our Lord."
- Philippians 4:4–6 (NIV): "Rejoice in

the Lord always. I will say it again: Rejoice! Let your gentleness be evident to all. The Lord is near. Do not be anxious about anything, but in every situation, by prayer and petition, with thanksgiving, present your requests to God."

- Ephesians 3:17–19 (NLT): "Then Christ will make his home in your hearts as you trust in him. Your roots will grow down into God's love and keep you strong. And may you have the power to understand, as all God's people should, how wide, how long, how high, and how deep his love is. May you experience the love of Christ, though it is too great to understand fully. Then you will be made complete with all the fullness of life and power that comes from God."

- Ephesians 3:20–21 (NLT): "Now all glory to God, who is able, through his mighty power at work within us, to accomplish infinitely more than we might ask or think. Glory to him in the church and in Christ Jesus through all generations forever and ever! Amen."

- James 1:2–4 (NASB): "Consider it all joy, my brethren, when you encounter various trials, knowing that the testing of your faith produces endurance. And let endurance have its perfect result, so that you may be perfect and complete, lacking in nothing."

Six:
And in His Heart . . .

A good man brings good things out
of the good stored up in his heart,
and an evil man brings evil things out
of the evil stored up in his heart. For
the mouth speaks what the heart is full of.
— LUKE 6:44–46

Recently I saw a sign that made me laugh.
It read, "I dream of a better world where a
chicken can cross the road without having
their motives questioned."

Too funny.

But that kind of world can never exist for
the storyteller. For me as a writer, and for
you as the teller of your own stories, understanding the motivations of each character
is important. This helps keep their actions
and reactions in line with who they are. Let
me give you an example.

In my new book, *The Inn at Rose Harbor,*
Jo Marie buys a local bed-and-breakfast inn.

On the surface, it looks like an interesting entrepreneurial move. If the local newspaper came in to do a business piece on her, they might focus on a businesswoman and former bank executive making a gutsy move in a challenging economy. But in order to craft a story, I needed to know Jo Marie's backstory and understand what she really wanted. She'd inherited her mother's gift of hospitality, so on the surface, a bed-and-breakfast seems like the perfect place to start over after the death of her husband, Paul. They had been married less than a year, but Jo Marie understands that her life has been changed forever when she receives word that Paul has been killed in Afghanistan. She's surprised to discover he's left a large insurance policy, but that's just like him. All her friends urge her not to make any major changes until at least a year after Paul's death, but she can't face the empty life ahead of her.

When she comes to Cedar Cove to tour the bed-and-breakfast, she decides to buy it the moment she steps inside. Without understanding Jo Marie's motivation, this kind of reaction would make no sense at all. If she was indeed a gutsy businesswoman, as the newspaper may have written, would she really have made a snap decision about so momentous a move?

It wouldn't make sense — except that the reader already knows about Paul's death and that Jo Marie has not been able to feel settled since she received word of his death. When she steps into the inn, she immediately feels a sense of peace come over her. She knows she has found a sanctuary. That's why she renames the inn Rose Harbor Inn — rose after Paul Rose and harbor for the place she decides to set her anchor as the storms of life battered her.

Because the reader knows that more than anything, this young, grieving widow longs for peace and a sense of security, the spur-of-the-moment decision makes all the sense in the world. The fun, of course, comes in when with each guest, that sense of peace is challenged.

DISCOVERING DIFFERENT STROKES

In chapter 4 I talked about digging deeper. One of the ways we do that in a story is to explore motivation. In writing, it's necessary to find out what's behind every action of the character. And it's one of the things we do in our own lives that helps us understand those around us. Gary Chapman's popular book *The Five Love Languages* explores the underlying motivations or character traits that explain why a person, especially a spouse, communicates love in a certain way. It helps us to understand how an individual may want to receive love. Chapman identifies five different "love languages." Some people express their love in words. They want to talk about things and they want the person who loves them to do so as well. He calls this language "Words of Affirmation."

Another person may express love and wish to receive it in what Chapman calls "Quality Time." This person values undivided attention — the gift of time spent together.

Still another love language is "Receiving Gifts." We've all known those people who delight in buying and giving the perfect gift. They also see the gifts given to them as signs of love.

Other people express their love in "Acts of Service." They may never be able to say the words, but they are constantly doing things to show love.

"Physical Touch" is another one of Chapman's love languages. The person who speaks this language prefers hugging, kissing, hand holding, or even a warm handshake.

As we get to know each person's heart and discover their love language, we set the stage for understanding a number of communication difficulties, as well as being able to identify couples who are "made for each other." Just think of the conflict that may arise between a couple if one person craves quality time, say, and the other gives acts of service. A husband may be off washing and buffing his wife's car while she's sitting home, longing for nothing more than her husband at her side. All the while he's away doing what he feels is the perfect expression of his love.

In my life, my love language is Words of Affirmation, while Wayne speaks Quality Time. By knowing this about each other we've each come to appreciate the gifts offered by the other in a whole new way.

WHY DO THEY BEHAVE LIKE THAT?

With any character, whether a main character or a secondary character, one of the most important things to discover is why they do what they do. What motivates them? When I'm writing a book, if I don't know the impetus behind the actions of each character, those actions won't ring true.

Actions reveal so much about a character. It reminds me of the story of a shoe company that decided to further expand their market. They sent two salesmen to different regions of the Australian outback. After some time, headquarters received a telegram from each salesman. The first said, "No business here — (Stop) — Aborigines don't wear shoes." The second read, "Huge opportunity — (Stop) — Aborigines don't wear shoes." It is easy to spot the pessimist — the glass-half-empty sort of person — and the optimist in this story. Each acted completely in character.

It's the same in life. We can usually tell immediately when someone in our family acts "out of character." It immediately raises red flags for us. The more we are able to understand the people around us, the easier it is to accept their actions and to love them.

ASKING WHY

We go even deeper to learn why a character is the way he is. As a writer, I keep asking the relentless *why*, followed by *what if?* Why did my hero walk away from that fight? Why does my heroine need to check and double-check the locks on the door every time she goes out?

Once, while conducting a workshop, I asked the participants how their heroine would react to a spider on the kitchen countertop. Their answers were most telling. One had her heroine scream and call for help.

Another gently scooted the spider onto a piece of paper and carefully deposited it outdoors. And another quickly swept the spider into the kitchen sink, turned on the water until it was down the drain, and then reached for the garbage disposal switch.

Two people may act the very same way, enough so that a person observing the action could conclude that they are exactly alike. And usually nothing could be further from the truth. When I'm home in Port Orchard, I wake early in the morning so that I have time to do my Bible reading, journal writing, and devotionals and still get to the local high school swimming pool in time to swim laps with a wonderful group of friends who love the smell of chlorine in the morning as much as I do. I've been swimming laps for over twenty years now. An outside observer might see me and the other swimmers there at six in the morning, all donning swim caps and easing into the water. If he's a high school student, he may not see the twenty-plus-years difference between my age and the octogenarians who swim with me. Perhaps he concludes that we are looking to fill our retirement days with an activity. Because we are using the high school pool, he may imagine we have limited resources and avail ourselves of this pool even though it means we have to come at what might appear to him to be an ungodly hour. He may even think it seems kind of sad that we don't horse around and have fun instead of getting to work completing our laps.

This imaginary student didn't dig deep enough, and because he didn't, his conclusions are wrong. I swim before starting a full day in which I'll write a predetermined number of manuscript pages, connect with my agent or my publicist, and manage a staff of six. I might have a lengthy discussion with my editor or my publisher. I might have meetings on a variety of subjects. In a single day I am often required to make so many decisions that by midafternoon my head is spinning. I might rush home from that pool to quickly do my hair in time for a video shoot or a meeting with some of the Seattle Seahawks (my favorite team) about charity possibilities. Despite what my imaginary student might think after a casual observation, my life is far from empty. It's the same for my fellow swimmers as well.

He was wrong about limited resources, too. If I chose to, I could have a pool built at our home so that I wouldn't have to leave the house, get in the car, and drive to the high school pool every morning.

So why do I do it?

Over the years the adult swimmers have become my friends. Pool time with them is one of the touchstones of my life. Every Christmas I prepare a special tea for these special friends. We've made it a practice to arrive at the pool ten or so minutes before it formally opens and wait together in the lobby, chatting and visiting. But once the doors open, it's serious business. We can't wait to get into the water and start our workout. I can see the difference regular exercise has made in our health, too. When someone can reach the age of eighty or ninety and move with the grace of someone many years younger, that inspires me. And seeing that this routine and regular exercise keeps our minds just as nimble has made me a believer.

Besides, I've been a fish ever since I was nine years old. One of my favorite pictures of me as a kid was taken when I was about four or five. I'm standing in the middle of a wading pool with the water barely above my ankles. My arms are spread wide like wings and there is a look of sublime joy on my face. It's as if I'm saying to the world, "Look at me." Swimming was one of those seeds God planted in my life that has continued to grow.

The point of this is to show how superficial judgments can lead to faulty conclusions. When it comes to examining the motivations of the people and circumstances in your own life, don't make the mistake of forming quick and sometimes faulty assumptions. Very often there's a lot more to it.

MAKING CHOICES

Another way we explore motivations and dig deeper is through examining the choices a character — or a person — makes. Think about it: every time we make a choice, we show who we are. In the example I gave at the beginning of this chapter, Jo Marie shows us what she is made of, even in the throes of deep grief. Rather than continue her comfortable life in Seattle as an upwardly mobile banking professional, she reaches for a challenge, a choice that helps her deal with her grief. That decision tells us something about her.

Both Wayne and I are working hard to stay fit. We each bought a little meter called a FitBit. This tiny device totals our steps every day. Because I have a sedentary job I rarely get in my ten thousand steps a day, but I average a good six to seven thousand, and on good days manage to meet my goal. For the last several weeks we've been challenging each other to do better, to be more active. Wayne is actually far more athletic than I am. He regularly plays golf and bikes, but he was laid low recently by a shoulder surgery. Because Wayne's been tied up doing a lot of physical therapy, I've bested him quite a bit recently. Naturally I make sure he knows I've outdone him. He hasn't taken kindly to that, and a good-natured competition has arisen. I laughed when I caught him trying to place his FitBit on Bogie, our very active little dog. It was too funny but it just shows how determined he was to find a way to best me. There's nothing like a little competition to keep us moving.

PUSHING BUTTONS

One of the best ways to develop plot is to place a character in a situation where his or her buttons are pushed. Like my example earlier of the spider on the kitchen countertop, the character's actions reveal who he or she really is.

Being a sports fan, I can attest to the fact that a game is never more fun than when your team is up against the wall and comes out fighting. That's when you see what your team is made of.

It's the same with the people in our lives.

Those who know how best to push our buttons do so in order to rile us enough that we reveal our weaknesses. In life, this is where we sometimes fail because those we love know how to get under our skin faster and better than anyone else. They don't need to think twice when it comes to saying or doing the one thing that irritates us most . . . the one thing that is sure to get a rise out of us. I once heard someone say that family is about loving each other at the top of our lungs. It's true. We often don't know we have hidden anger or resentment to root out until someone hits us where it hurts. And then, by heaven, watch out.

Besides pushing buttons, some of the other things that can often reveal hidden motivations are family secrets, a character's worst fear, his greatest hope, or even his biggest dream. If you get stuck in the telling of your own story, stop for a moment and examine what it is that's preventing you from moving forward. What has happened in your life that's preventing you from examining the past? What is it about the people in your life? Or perhaps it's something about yourself that needs perusal. The key to this, naturally, is to know yourself. And you know what? We need to know God in order to know ourselves, and we do that by digging into His Word, by listening to Him, by spending time with Him on a regular basis.

Reading Between the Lines

Sometimes discovering the story behind the story requires reading between the lines. For the last year I've been reading a devotional that gives background on the hymns and hymn writers, highlighting events that led to the songs that have withstood the test of time. These are the songs with deep spiritual depth and theology that resonate with the soul. I love singing the praise songs, but the hymns of yesteryear — "The Old Rugged Cross," "What a Friend We Have in Jesus," "Amazing Grace" — will always remain some of my favorites.

One I read about recently was the children's song "Jesus Loves Me," written by Anna Bartlett Warner. I learned that Anna and her sister taught Bible study classes to the cadets at West Point for many years. When Anna died in 1915, she was so loved by the staff and cadets that she was buried with military honors.

What stood out in my mind, however, while reading this devotional was a sort of postscript — a one-line sentence regarding an incident from 1972. At the time, Communist China was still closed to the world. Chinese Christians were persecuted and faith in Christ was banned. All outgoing mail was strictly censored. However, one letter mailed by a Chinese Christian passed inspection. It simply said that the "This I Know" society was alive and well. The message was taken from the childlike line from the song Anna Warner composed to teach children about Jesus: "Jesus loves me, this I know."

Through the years when China was closed to the world, these faithful Christians found a way to inform the outside world that their love for Jesus remained strong and their faith in Him hadn't faltered. They were able to bear witness to their character — to what continued to motivate them — by inserting one cryptic phrase between the lines.

It's the same for us. Sometimes we will find the motivating force of those "characters" around us only by reading between the lines. It keeps coming back to digging deep.

WHAT DO WE WANT?

Writers will tell you that one of the most important questions we ask is, "What does my character want?" If we know what he wants, we know how to create conflict (by making it difficult for him to obtain) or keep tensions high by withholding the very thing he wants.

As we tell our stories, a strategy that might not take long is to create a list that answers the question. Think about your own life. What is it you want? It isn't as easy to identify as it might sound. If I asked you to write down five things that you really want (and told you you couldn't write down "world peace") it probably wouldn't take you very long to hand me back a list that skims the surface. My guess is you'd say:

Good health for me and my family
To be out of debt
To be happy
To find fulfillment in my work
To have a closer relationship with God

The truth is we all want those same things. Health addresses the physical. Seeking to be debt free is about the financial. When we ask to be happy, we're talking about the emotional. Finding fulfillment in work seeks to satisfy both a mental and an emotional need. And looking to have a closer relationship with God speaks to that spiritual hunger we have. These are all good desires. But I believe we are complex beings, and there are other desires, dreams we've been afraid to voice. It was certainly that way with me when I held onto the hope of one day being a writer. I didn't dare tell my family or friends because it seemed like such an unattainable dream.

Think about your own desires and try again, digging deep. If there wasn't a single obstacle blocking your path, what would you be doing? Recently I accepted this challenge myself and made a list of five things that seemed completely beyond the realm of possibility for me. These dreams are so big that when I mentioned the first one to Wayne, he grabbed at his heart and staggered backward. What I loved most about this exercise is that I know there is nothing within my own power I can do to make this list a reality. If any one thing on this list comes to pass I will know it came directly from God.

What was it on my list that caused Wayne to grab at his heart? I want the ability to give away ten million dollars in one year to further God's kingdom on earth. Ten million . . . Oh, and since I was dreaming very big, I put down owning part or all of the Seattle Seahawks football franchise. Why not? We serve an amazing God.

WHAT'S BEHIND WHAT WE WANT?

Let's get back to your story. If you were to make a list of five audacious goals, what would they be? Don't be afraid. Dig deeper. Take the desire to be debt free as an example. What do you suppose is behind that need? Perhaps you have a deep-seated need for security and any kind of debt is uncomfortable. Or maybe you're deeply in debt and your pride won't let anyone else help, even though you're one step away from disaster. As we keep digging, we understand ourselves more and more. And that digging reveals new truths whether it's about a character in a story or about us personally, living our very own stories.

Sometimes it feels emotionally painful to talk about going beyond the surface. After all, it can be pretty uncomfortable to reveal the desires of our hearts. Rose-colored glasses and all. But if we are serious about telling our stories and we want to follow the Lord's example, we can't shy away from examining our hearts. He didn't. "Immediately Jesus knew in His spirit that this was what they were thinking in their hearts, and He said to them, 'Why are you thinking these things?' " (Mark 2:7–9).

Answer the question: what is it you truly want? Try to get to some of your deepest motivations. See if you can unpeel the layers and find out what's at the core. One of the tricks to going deeper is to keep telling yourself over and over, "That's good, but what else?"

The Narrator

As we begin to tell our story, we need to examine who the narrator is. Remember reading *The Great Gatsby* in high school and having discussions about the narrator, Nick Carraway? In many ways he was more important than Daisy and Gatsby, because we watched the story unfold through his eyes.

It's the same with our stories. They are told through our own narration, and sometimes that narrator is not reliable. We often tell ourselves things that are damaging, and these things can creep into our stories. Listen to yourself as you talk. Do you say things like, "I'm not very good at . . . ," or "I've never been able to . . . ," or "I was always clumsy and nothing will ever change that"?

I grew up under a cloud of dire prophecy.

107

I remember hearing my third-grade teacher tell my mother, "Debbie is a sweet little girl, but she'll never do well in school." When I finally got up the nerve to share my dream of writing, another teacher told me, "You can't write, Debbie. Why, you can't even spell." And who could ever forget the words, "Let's just go straight to the Chubby Department, Debbie. They're sure to have your size there." It took me years of examining those narrations and refuting them one by one to get past them. That's why I cheered for Aibileen in the book *The Help* when she gathered little Mae Mobley in her arms and had her repeat, "You is kind, you is smart, you is important." Aibileen knew the value of speaking truth into this emotionally battered little girl's life.

God's Word emphasizes this as well in Proverbs 23:7a: "For as he thinks in his heart, so *is* he." As you tell your story, examine parts of it that may have slipped into your telling. Is that true? Who told you that? Try to see your story from God's perspective. If you've always felt that you were somehow deficient, get to know the God who delights in you. That's right, He used the word *delight.* "The LORD delights in those who fear him, who put their hope in his unfailing love" (Ps. 147:11). Make sure your story reflects that.

Seven:
And It Came to Pass . . .

Brothers and sisters, I do not consider
myself yet to have taken hold of it. But
one thing I do: Forgetting what is behind
and straining toward what is ahead, I
press on toward the goal to win the prize
for which God has called me heavenward
in Christ Jesus.
— PHILIPPIANS 3:13–14

When we think about story, the first thing
that comes to mind is plot. Simply put, the
plot is the what-happens-next of the story.
If you've ever eavesdropped while two little
girls play Barbie dolls together, you'll
recognize plot. As each girl hops those spiky
little high-heeled Barbie feet along the floor
you can hear their alternating high-pitched
voices:

"Pretend she picked up the dog and
started to walk away —" says one as she
squeezes a tiny stuffed dog under her Bar-

bie's arm.

"But I wouldn't let you because it was my dog and she didn't have permission —" The second Barbie tries to poke the dog out from under Barbie number one's arm, followed by the sound of hard vinyl bouncing off hard vinyl as two angry Barbies tussle over the dog.

"And when you dropped the dog, I picked it up —" Said dog is again stuffed under Barbie's arm.

"But the dog ran away."

This kind of plot building goes on as long as the players are prepared to play or until one of the Barbies loses her head and needs to go to the pretend hospital.

Plot, like serious Barbie action, refers to the series of events that comprise a story. Sometimes the story is told in a chronological fashion, starting at the beginning and moving through a sequence of events until the final culminating scene. At other times the story is told by starting somewhere in the middle, perhaps where the most compelling action takes place, and then working backward, weaving in the backstory through a series of flashbacks occasionally interrupting the forward story.

MY FIVE ELEMENTS OF STORY

The challenge I set for myself long ago was to have five elements in each story I write. First, I want the story to be *provocative* — my goal is to make my readers think. My 2011 book *A Turn in the Road* is a good example of this. If you were to take a lengthy road trip, where would you drive, and who would you choose to travel with you? Or another book, *Twenty Wishes,* asks, If you were making a list, what would you wish? I want to provoke my reader to apply what's happening in this fictional tale to his or her own life.

I also want my story to be *relevant.* If what's happening in the plot doesn't reflect my readers' lives, there is no point in writing it. I have always enjoyed getting reader feedback and, in fact, have sought it. One comment I've gotten again and again from my readers is that my characters feel so real to them. They know someone just like so-and-so. Or they tell me that something similar to the situation in my book has happened to a friend of theirs. My story ideas come from everyday life, from things I've read or people I've met. Relevant.

The next one is important. I want my books to be *entertaining.* I don't ever want to lose sight of the fact that when a reader purchased my book, she was also committing to a block of time to read it. I never want anyone to come away disappointed. I don't use my books as a political platform or to show how well I've done my research. I write a good story, hopefully a riveting one that keeps the reader entertained. The message must be subtle.

The fourth element I strive for is *creativity*. I want to pour creativity into the telling — in the story itself and in the way I tell it. Probably the most creative book I've ever written is titled *Between Friends*. I used a unique storytelling device and didn't use one word of dialogue or one word of description. The story is the tale of a lifelong friendship between two women. It's told as if the reader is leafing through the pages of a scrapbook. With each book I strive to find a way to do something unique or different.

The final element I like to add to every story is *realism* or honesty. It's far too easy to tie all the story detail up in a neat bow and write, "The End," and leave the reader scratching her head, wondering how this or that could have possibly happened. For example, in many books a hero and heroine can argue and bicker through an entire manuscript and then in the last chapter suddenly declare their love for one another. The emotional turnaround is enough to give a reader whiplash. I'm afraid I've been guilty of this myself, in the early years of my writing career. The story must ring true, and the conclusion has to live up to the promise set up early in the book.

I apply those five elements to every story I write.

That's why I spend a good deal of time plotting each book. Once I have the basic premise — the idea that sparks my attention — I begin to play with it. I start by taking a piece of paper and listing twenty to forty incidents that could happen. I do this in brainstorming fashion, because at this stage I want these ideas to be organic. I find that the less I try to orchestrate at this stage, the more inventive the ideas will be.

Once I have some story ideas, I flesh out the characters. Since I often write ensemble fiction — following multiple story lines that weave together around a common theme — I'll usually choose three or four characters and begin to explore who they are, what they want, and what they are most afraid of. It's important to uncover some of their underlying motivations. As I explained earlier, when I weave different plots together, it's much like braiding hair. Although there are three strands, they make one long, unified braid.

Once I have the characters, I examine each one and decide how best to challenge them. We're going to talk about conflict and challenge in chapter 14, but for now let me just say that nothing moves a story — a plot — along faster than giving the characters challenges.

WHAT IF . . .

Picture a Jacqueline Kennedy–like character. Let's say her name *is* Jacqueline. She adores her only child, Paul — a rising star in corporate banking — for whom she has always harbored the highest hopes. Now, what happens if that son falls in love with Tammie Lee, who comes from the swamps of who-knows-where? The wedding is bad enough. Paul calls Tammie Lee his little Southern belle, but Jacqueline can't even keep track of all of Tammie Lee's cousins and kinfolk. She had pictured a wedding with collard greens and grits and half expected deep-fried Twinkies in place of the traditional wedding cake. Okay, it wasn't as bad as she'd imagined, but Tammie Lee's Southern sweetness is more than Jacqueline can stomach. Why oh why can't Paul see that this marriage is a horrible mistake? When Jacqueline finds out Tammie Lee is pregnant within a few months of the wedding, she's horrified. It would be easy for Jacqueline to walk away from Tammie Lee, but — here's the rub — Jacqueline's greatest fear is losing her son. That element is what moves the plot forward. She has to find a way to connect with Tammie Lee if she wants her son in her life. That challenge turned out to be Jacqueline Donovan's story line in *The Shop on Blossom Street.*

Applying those what-if scenarios to our stories is what helps us get to the very core of what our characters want most and what they fear most. It's almost like when we apply some worst-case scenario thinking to our own lives.

ACTION AND REACTION

In plotting, it's not just what happens that moves the story along; it's how the characters react to what happens. It's the same in our own real-life stories. Good things and bad things happen to all of us. The power of the story is in how we react to them.

It's like the story of Joseph from the Bible. He grew up in a house full of brothers — there were twelve sons in all and he was the second youngest — but hands down, he was the favorite. His father, Jacob, made no secret of his preference. In fact, while the other sons wore sturdy, serviceable clothes, Jacob had an expensive, ornate multicolored coat made for Joseph. The coat proclaimed his father's favoritism every time Joseph put his arms into the sleeves. Apparently, Joseph had an arrogant streak to go with his most-favored-son status.

In ancient Canaan there was little more important than receiving a father's blessing. Joseph's standing with his father as the favorite became the envy of all his brothers. Even if Joseph had never uttered a word, his brothers would have been consumed with jealousy. The Bible tells us they hated him. Now, *hate* is a very strong word.

But Joseph possessed an unusual gift. He dreamed dreams that were prophetic, and he had the ability to understand what those dreams meant. One particular morning he woke from a vivid dream. He relayed it to his brothers, since it concerned them. He said:

"Listen to this dream I had: We were binding sheaves of grain out in the field when suddenly my sheaf rose and stood upright, while your sheaves gathered around mine and bowed down to it."

His brothers said to him, "Do you intend to reign over us? Will you actually rule us?" And they hated him all the more because of his dream and what he had said.

Then he had another dream, and he told it to his brothers. "Listen," he said, "I had another dream, and this time the sun and moon and eleven stars were bowing down to me."

When he told his father as well as his brothers, his father rebuked him and said, "What is this dream you had? Will your mother and I and your brothers actually come and bow down to the ground before you?" His brothers were jealous of him, but his father kept the matter in mind.

— GENESIS 37:5–10

Those dreams were the straw that broke the proverbial camel's back when it came to Joseph's relationship with his brothers. The ten hatched a plan to kill him, but at the last minute decided instead to sell him to a nomadic tribe for a handful of silver shekels.

The brothers kept his offending coat, ripped it, and smeared it with blood to make it look as if wild animals had attacked Joseph. In the meantime, Joseph was resold to a captain of the Pharaoh's guard in Egypt. The Bible says that the Lord prospered everything Joseph did. The plot took several twists and turns and Joseph saw trouble as well as redemption. Remember what I mentioned earlier in talking about the book of Ruth, how the Hebrew word *wayehi* literally means, "Trouble is on the horizon but redemption is coming"? That was true for the story of Joseph's captivity and eventual promotion to the pharaoh's second-in-command.

This is one of those edge-of-the-seat stories. (You can read it for yourself in Genesis, chapters 37–50.) The most important part of the story is Joseph's reaction to his brothers' treachery and to all the trouble he encountered. His youthful arrogance was replaced by maturity, courage, and mercy. Rather than grow bitter, Joseph saw God's hand in the story. In Genesis 50:20, speaking to his brothers, he sums it up: "You intended to harm me, but God intended it for good to accomplish what is now being done, the saving of many lives."

That's the kind of reaction that marks a hero who sees his story as a journey with an ultimate purpose. And it's a powerful example of how God wants us to view the plot points of our own lives. What may have been intended for harm, God used for good.

TENSION AND PACING

When I'm plotting a novel, I pay close attention to the pacing. A storyteller knows about keeping listeners or readers on the edge of their seats. We do this by keeping tension in the story. One of the tricks of our trade is to end each chapter with a cliffhanger. I want my books to be so compelling that readers are tempted to stay up all night simply because they find the story so entertaining they can't stop until they reach the end of the book.

It reminds me of the letter I received from a loyal reader who said she loved my books. "They put me to sleep every night." I'm glad I understood what she meant, or her words might have given me pause.

But most readers will look at the clock and promise themselves they'll only read to the end of the chapter. Picture us writers with a twinkle in our collective eyes as we plan to make it almost impossible to put that book down at the end of a chapter.

My goal as a writer is to leave the reader wanting more.

As we tell our own stories, the tension will come naturally if we don't sanitize the telling. Trouble will come. We just need to keep in mind that redemption isn't far behind, although it might not seem that way.

Another important part of plot is the twist, an unexpected detour. As I told the Joseph story above, I left out some of the twists that make the story even more compelling. But add in a treacherous woman's false accusation; an unwarranted fall from grace, including a prison stint; and a miraculous restoration by Pharaoh — and all the honors that go with it — and you'll have some of the twists and turns in Joseph's story.

You won't have to look hard to find those unexpected detours in stories or in your own life. As I write this, neighborhoods all across this country have homes in foreclosure due to the housing crisis. Families have had the financial rug pulled out from under them. I'm praying that in time, when those stories are told, the people who suffered this unexpected twist will be able to say what Joseph said: "You intended to harm me, but God intended it for good."

STORY ARC

The plot of a story does not look like a timeline — like a straight horizontal line. We call it a story arc because the story usually starts in one place, swells in tension and conflict (sometimes called rising action), comes to a climax, and then tapers back down (descending action). In my stories, as we near the end, all the different story lines begin to intertwine. I think of it almost like knitting a sweater. All the pieces are there, and then comes the time when they are joined. If you first looked at the sleeve and then the side, you might wonder how the two pieces would ever come together, but once all the pieces are laid out it's easy to see.

I opened this chapter with Philippians 3:13–14 because the verse mirrors that arc, that journey. We press on toward the end, toward the prize. The tension is there as we strain forward to capture the promised treasure. We're pressing toward the happily ever after.

All of that may seem like more information about plot than you ever wanted to know, but the reason I share each part is that the story of our lives involves an intricate plot as well. I think that understanding how story moves forward gives us an insight into how God is plotting our own stories. It helps us recognize the pacing, tension, twists, and turns in our lives as more than catastrophes. Each event — disaster or delight — is part of the plot, moving our story along.

■ ■ ■ ■

Storytelling Prompt

If you were to plot your life out from beginning to end on a timeline, list what would be some of the high points and low points. If you feel ambitious, create the actual timeline. Have there been times when your life became too complicated? Describe those times. Can you identify the arcs? How did you get through those thickly plotted seasons?

The Hero's Journey

We can't talk about plot and story without exploring the *hero's journey.* Storytellers have long known there is a natural pattern for telling a story, but in 1946 mythologist Joseph Campbell first described the model of the hero's journey and assigned progressive steps to it in his book *The Hero with a Thousand Faces.* From ancient mythic tales like Homer's *Odyssey* to modern Hollywood's *Star Wars* or *Lord of the Rings,* most stories follow this familiar archetype. For natural storytellers like me, it's something we've instinctively understood and incorporated into our stories. If you're like me and grew up reading, you'll recognize this pattern.

Since Campbell first identified this mono-myth — or cyclical journey — there have been a number of variations on the steps used to describe the journey. Often it's divided into eight steps:

1. **The call** — the invitation offered to the hero to enter the adventure.
2. **The threshold** — the jumping-off point for the adventure. The hero will encounter guardians who may block his path, stepping aside only when the hero is prepared to meet the challenge of the journey.
3. **The challenges** — the hero faces a series of challenges or temptations. These often become more difficult along the way. This step requires the hero to figure out who may try to lead him astray. Much of a book is made up of this step — challenge after challenge. And much of our lives seems taken up by this step.
4. **The abyss** — here is where the challenge is so great that the hero must surrender completely to the adventure, usually to face his great-

est fear.

5. **The transformation** — the hero has conquered the abyss and overcome his fears.

6. **The revelation** — a sudden, dramatic change in the way the hero thinks or views life. Change is crucial in order for him to become a new person.

7. **The atonement** — the hero accepts his new identity.

8. **The return** — upon his return, the hero may have discovered his gifts, skills, or a new awareness.

Joseph Campbell believed that the hero's journey allowed everyday people to identify their own heroic adventure, their strengths and their weaknesses. He observed that all human beings face a series of trials that allow us to grow and to find our place in this world.

Sound familiar? We can track much of our journey through life in terms of the archetypal hero's journey, especially our spiritual journey. Or we can look to the life journey of other family members — our parents or grandparents. We can examine what happened when they conquered life's trials, or

how they developed confidence and perspective. Their journeys transformed them
and us, changing us all through the adversity
that they faced.

If you've plotted your life, or even created
a timeline, it might be an interesting exercise
to examine what you find in the light of the
hero's journey — from the first call to the
return.

EIGHT:
HE TUCKED THE TREASURE DEEP IN HIS SACK . . .

Then He said to them, "Therefore every scribe instructed concerning the kingdom of heaven is like a householder who brings out of his treasure things new and old."
— MATTHEW 13:52 (KJV)

Isn't it strange that our treasures — our stuff — can say so much about us? When I'm writing a book and I describe rooms or possessions, those are always clues to the character. Like the fireplace in the three-sided shed in *The Inn at Rose Harbor,* where Jo Marie finds refuge with her knitting, or the knitted baby blanket representing each character's struggle in the book *The Shop on Blossom Street.*

These telling treasures are not limited to my fiction. If you were to walk through my office and take the stairs up to my writing loft, you'd learn several things about me on

127

the journey. I have an autograph collection arranged on the walls leading up to the space where I do the majority of my writing. Each day I'm inspired by authors whose work I've admired my entire life. The fact that the carpet is slightly worn in the center of the steps speaks to my commitment to spending time nearly every day doing what I love and am so grateful to be able to do — that is, writing my own books. Even more of my autograph collection is on display in my home. There's a yarn room and a big, sunny kitchen. So much of what I love is part of my everyday environment — family, Christmas, my faith, food, knitting, writing.

If you visited that home in Port Orchard at Christmastime, you'd learn even more about me. I have several decorated Christmas trees. We gather gifts for each of my children's families under their own tree. You'll find multiple nativity scenes in every room. I'm guessing you are the same way: if you look around your own home you too will discover tangible hints of who you are and what you love.

When we are telling our stories, we need to look at the treasures of our lives and find a way to wind them into the telling. They usually speak volumes about us. These treasures come in many forms. Perhaps they are the symbols of our lives, or actual things — artifacts — or letters, lists, or journals. Let's take a look at some of those elements.

SYMBOLS

Remember back in your high school and college literature classes when you had to analyze symbolism in stories? Light and dark in *The Scarlet Letter*. Ralph and his conch shell in *Lord of the Flies*. Blood in *Macbeth*. We writers often use symbolism to add a layer of complexity to our stories. For instance, in my books, knitting is often the symbolic coming together of characters.

The Bible is filled with symbolism. That's what makes it such a fascinating read, whether it is your first time to read through it or your thirtieth time. I'm always learning something new. The stones piled as an altar to mark God's mighty works. The blood sacrifices of the Old Testament foreshadowing Christ and the ultimate sacrifice. The feasts. It would take more than one lifetime to unravel all the symbolism and richness.

What about your own life? Are there symbols that play into your story? For me, there are several. One is a hospital door I was told to go through when I was visiting my terminally ill cousin. It said ABSO-LUTELY NO ADMITTANCE. At first I was confused, but as I pushed open that door it became a symbol of how I would choose to walk through life. Life is too short. I decided I'd no longer live my life cowering, afraid I would fail if I even tried to write and sell a novel. Instead, I would boldly walk through the most impossible doors.

Another symbol in my life is the cameo. If you've met me in person or seen photos of me, most likely I was wearing a cameo. They are exquisite works of art, but they are so much more. The cameo is made out of a stone or a seashell that has two planes of different colors. The top layer is carved away, leaving an image in a color that contrasts with the base color. Some of the finest sculptors have carved in this style. It's a metaphor, a symbol, for my life — painstakingly carving away all the bits and pieces that don't belong until the real design begins to show. In many ways, this is what God has done for me, chipping away the pieces that distract from the woman He longs for me to be, so bit by bit I am shaped into His image.

For me, the book is another symbol. From the moment that first book was placed in my hands at a young age, I knew: one day I would write stories like this. Writing is my joy, my passion. The book itself is a symbol of that passion and of the power of story. I often find myself absently stroking a book's cover in my hands as I speak. It's a symbol that is threaded throughout my life.

My box of family recipes is another symbol in my life. These recipes are about so much more than mere sustenance. My recipe box represents what has connected my family through the generations. It is comfort. When times are rough or when I need to cocoon, I cook. It is service — something I do as a gift for those I love. It is a creative outlet. I relish finding new recipes and tweaking old ones, but nothing beats those recipes handed down in our family. So many of our family get-togethers centered around food. That box represents the large family gatherings of my childhood, with aunts and cousins sharing recipes. And it continues in the celebrations we now have with kids and grandchildren.

ARTIFACTS

Archeologists understand the importance of our treasures. They study ancient cultures by discovering and studying physical evidence — whether treasures or tools, graves or dwellings, temples or humble caves. Those who study history and culture spend their lives uncovering treasures of bygone societies. The Minoan society of Ancient Greece would have been completely forgotten if not for the artifacts they left behind. The Minoan people, whose language to this day cannot be interpreted, left behind symbols of who they were and how they lived, giving us a window into their everyday lives and an opportunity to understand their culture.

Have you ever watched the PBS television program *Antiques Roadshow*? It's fascinating to watch history unwind through a collection of letters or paintings. My husband is an avid Civil War historian, so our favorite segments are the ones that include a whole collection of artifacts, say, a Civil War canteen, a regimental flag, a rifle, a letter with the signature of one of the storied Civil War heroes, and daguerreotypes of the ancestor who originally owned the items. We're always fascinated to hear the expert tell how the collection can be authenticated as he works through each piece, comparing dates and stories. What to some would look like a box of old stuff ends up being valued as a priceless, museum-worthy treasure that tells part of the story of a dark time in our nation's history. This story is told not through a written journal, but through a box of treasures.

Take a look through your family treasures. What do they tell you? How about your own artifacts? Do you save movie ticket stubs? An old corsage? What do these treasures represent? What do they mean to you? As you dig through your own keepsakes, even more of your story will emerge.

LETTERS

There is nothing a writer or historian likes better than a stack of old letters or a journal. As I mentioned earlier, I wrote an entire book, *Between Friends,* using letters be-tween the two friends, diary entries, and newspaper clippings. No dialogue. No descriptions. No scenes. Yet my readers tell me the story came alive for them, and many consider it my best book to date.

In our own lives, saved letters give us another viewpoint. Have you ever come across letters between your parents? What an eye-opener those would be — to see Mom and Dad as a couple in love instead of as our parents. Or letters penned by famous people? The following are excerpts from a very long letter written by Ludwig van Beethoven in 1812 to an unidentified "Immortal Beloved":

My angel, my all, my own self — only

a few words today, and that too with pencil (with yours) — only till tomorrow is my lodging definitely fixed. What abominable waste of time in such things — why this deep grief, where necessity speaks?

Can our love persist otherwise than through sacrifices, than by not demanding everything? Canst thou change it, that thou are not entirely mine, I not entirely thine? Oh, God, look into beautiful Nature and compose your mind to the inevitable. Love demands everything and is quite right, so it is for me with you, for you with me — only you forget so easily, that I must live for you and for me — were we quite united, you would notice this painful feeling as little as I should . . .

What longing in tears for you — You — my Life — my All — farewell. Oh, go on loving me — never doubt the faithfullest heart

Of your beloved

L

Ever thine.
Ever mine.
Ever ours.[1]

Doesn't that resonate with the Beethoven

134

we know from his music? We learn more about his passions from his letter. And the ending . . . "Ever thine. Ever mine. Ever ours." How beautiful. Letters can offer a richer, deeper look into our stories.

LISTS

Another treasure often used to help tell a story is the simple list. My book *Twenty Wishes* starts with a list. Anne Marie finds herself alone as a recent widow with no children and no idea what she is to do next. Along with some friends, she decides to make a list of twenty wishes. Although she owns a successful bookstore, she is unhappy and depressed, so the very first thing on her list is "find one good thing about life."

She goes on to list other wishes, like learning to knit, finding something good to do for others, and, somehow, falling in love again. The list is the centerpiece of the story.

I'm a list person, so writing *Twenty Wishes* came naturally to me. In my nonfiction book *God's Guest List,* I tell about the list I made of thirty people I wanted to meet before I die. That list was such fun to create, but God had other plans. He let me know that He would graciously allow me to meet many of the people on my list, but that He also had a list of people He wanted me to meet. I needed to be on the lookout for those people He'd bring into my life without warning. I'm still working on that list.

As you tell your own story, don't forget the power of lists. One of my friends keeps a prayer journal in which she records her Bible reading and her prayer. She says it has become the most powerful tool in her life. Just looking over the lists of things for which she has prayed and then seeing the answers to those prayers has deepened her walk with God and helped her see the whole story. She says that by the time the answers have come, if she hadn't written down the original prayers, she might not have seen the connection.

JOURNALS

I've often used a diary in my books to reveal something about the character, as in the book *Susannah's Garden.* As Susannah's mother begins slipping away from her, Susannah finds her diary and learns something about her mother that she never knew.

Susannah stared at the diary, afraid she might learn things about her parents she'd rather not know — and yet she was intensely curious. It wasn't hers to read, she reminded herself. This was her mother's private property . . .

Susannah frowned. Her mother had wanted to be a nurse? This was news to her. In all her years of growing up, Susannah couldn't recollect one word about her mother having — or wanting — a career . . .[2]

By now you know that I value a journal for telling my story. My many journals are among my own treasures. I began journaling years ago, and there is a whole library of journals that tell the story of my life. When I take time to go back and read over them — to reflect on my life — I'm always surprised at how much I had forgotten and how much I learn by rereading them. They are not something I'd want to share with anyone else, since I write honestly and without holding anything back, but as I tell the story of my life, they are the raw material from which I work.

Whether you use artifacts, symbols, journals, lists, or whatever treasures are part of your life, these elements are an important part of the telling. Just as I use them when creating a story, you can use them as you piece together your own story. They are tools that recall and tell the story of your own life and open doors to understanding who you are and your life's purpose.

Storytelling Prompt

Make a list of important artifacts from your life — letters, treasures, books, mementos, photographs, and so on. Tell about one of those and what it represents.

The Scrapbook of Our Lives

Scrapbooking — the art of preserving photographs, documents, and mementos in order to tell family or personal history — has seen a rebirth in recent years. There are whole stores dedicated to the craft, and scrapbookers are creating some beautiful works of art as well as capturing family memories.

Scrapbooks originally rose to popularity in the fifteenth century, in a form they then called the "commonplace book." Later, especially during the Regency era, the "friendship album" took its place. And in Victorian times, the scrapbook came into its own when women pressed flowers and decorated the pages with their specimens, adding watercolor drawings and even locks of hair from friends and romantic interests.

Now that scrapbooking is again being practiced, many are finding it the perfect way to tell their stories and satisfy their creative spirits. Here are three suggestions for your scrapbooks:

1. Don't forget to add favorite Bible verses, bringing your spiritual heritage into your art.
2. Scrapbook with family members, so you'll be not only telling your story through your craft, but also creating memories at the same time.
3. Find ways to incorporate written stories along with the visual images. Too many photograph albums and scrapbooks don't tell the story in and of themselves — they need the creator to explain the photos. It renders them mute when the creator is no longer available.

NINE:
HE PICKED UP
THE SWORD . . .

God is not unjust; he will not forget your
work and the love you have shown him
as you have helped his people and
continue to help them.
— HEBREWS 6:10

In nearly every story there is a mission that
must be accepted or a journey that must be
begun. Some of the stories we like best are
the ones in which there is a reluctant hero
who has a mission thrust upon him.

One of the parables Jesus told has just
such a mission, with three different kinds of
heroes. Here's the story as He told it from
Matthew 25: 14–30:

Again, it will be like a man going on a
journey, who called his servants and
entrusted his wealth to them. To one he
gave five bags of gold, to another two
bags, and to another one bag, each ac-

cording to his ability. Then he went on his journey. The man who had received five bags of gold went at once and put his money to work and gained five bags more. So also, the one with two bags of gold gained two more. But the man who had received one bag went off, dug a hole in the ground and hid his master's money.

After a long time the master of those servants returned and settled accounts with them. The man who had received five bags of gold brought the other five. "Master," he said, "you entrusted me with five bags of gold. See, I have gained five more." His master replied, "Well done, good and faithful servant! You have been faithful with a few things; I will put you in charge of many things. Come and share your master's happiness!"

The man with two bags of gold also came. "Master," he said, "you entrusted me with two bags of gold; see, I have gained two more."

His master replied, "Well done, good and faithful servant! You have been faithful with a few things; I will put you in charge of many things. Come and share your master's happiness!"

Then the man who had received one bag of gold came. "Master," he said, "I knew that you are a hard man, harvesting where you have not sown and gathering where you have not scattered seed. So I was afraid and went out and hid your gold in the ground. See, here is what belongs to you."

His master replied, "You wicked, lazy servant! So you knew that I harvest where I have not sown and gather where I have not scattered seed? Well then, you should have put my money on deposit with the bankers, so that when I returned I would have received it back with interest.

"So take the bag of gold from him and give it to the one who has ten bags. For whoever has will be given more, and they will have an abundance. Whoever does not have, even what they have will be taken from them. And throw that worthless servant outside, into the darkness, where there will be weeping and gnashing of teeth."

The first two servants embraced the mission with enthusiasm. They must have seen it as a great opportunity. We don't have any details of what went on during the time the master was on his journey. Chances are there were many ups and down for our first two heroes. I'm guessing there were plenty of times when they worried over the risks they had taken. We know from the story that this master was a tough man. But in the end they accepted the mission, took the risk, and succeeded. Not only was the master happy with them, but he promised them even greater opportunities.

The third servant was the reluctant hero. In the end, because he refused the mission out of fear, he became an anti-hero. As he stood before the master holding the original bag of gold, probably caked with dirt, he admitted that he had been afraid to accept the mission. And because of his fear, there were consequences.

OUR TALENTS

In the parable above, called the Parable of the Talents, the version I've quoted calls the money the owner entrusts his servants with "bags of gold." In other versions, they are referred to as "talents." The talent, or *talanton,* was a variable denomination of coin, depending on the metal used.

You'll often hear a pastor or teacher talk about how much a talent is worth in today's value, but that is an impossible comparison, because the talent represents different denominations. The talents in this story may have been gold, silver, or copper — the original text did not specify. For that reason they could have been equal to as much as twenty years' wages.

Several biblical scholars think Jesus chose a nonspecific coinage on purpose because if we try to attach a specific value to these bags of treasure, we narrow the scope of the parable.

In modern English we use the word *talent* to refer to the skills and mental powers God has entrusted to us. I find that an interesting application of the parable. The Lord has entrusted all of us with different levels of skills, of talent, but He expects us to use these talents and return them with increase, rather than bury them.

As each of us begins to tell our story we need to explore the mission that has been set before us. I know I was given the gift of storytelling. How do I know? Because when I am telling a story there is such joy in the work. And because He has blessed the work of my hands. It reminds me of what the famous *Chariots of Fire* runner, Eric Liddell, said: "I believe God made me for a purpose, but He also made me fast. And when I run I feel His pleasure." I could say the same thing about writing. When I write, I feel God's pleasure. I feel joy, incredible happiness, and I know this is one reason He created me.

Is It Ever Too Late?

What happens if we reach our fifties, or even our sixties or seventies, and have not yet found our mission? Is it too late? Absolutely not! I know you've heard of Grandma Moses, who did not even start painting until the age of 76, when arthritis made her beloved embroidery impossible. By the time she died at age 101, she had created more than a thousand paintings.

I'll bet you didn't realize that Julia Child didn't begin her cooking career until after she turned 50 and wrote *Mastering the Art of French Cooking* with two of her Cordon Bleu classmates. She became the first important television chef, and many more have followed in her footsteps. Julia continued writing books and teaching the world to cook until her death at age 91.

Or take another writer, Laura Ingalls Wilder. She didn't write *Little House on the Prairie* until she was retirement age. In all, she wrote eight novels in that series, the last published as she turned 76. Her books have remained continuously in print and are considered classics of children's literature.

So the answer to the question "Is it ever too late?" is no. As you begin to see God's hand in your story, you're going to find the clues to your mission. Hopefully you picked up the sword long ago, but if not, never fear; it's never too late.

DOES A MISSION HAVE TO BE BIG?

In books and in movies we love to hear about ordinary people doing extraordinary things, but in real life we're often called to do small things over and over. My friend was telling me about the woman in her church who is the wedding coordinator. She's held the volunteer job for twenty or thirty years. Theirs is a beautiful, historic church, one in which many a bride has walked down the aisle. Do you know why the woman continues to perform this time-consuming, often nerve-racking job? She says that it is a way to welcome strangers into the fellowship of the church — to make them feel like it is their home. She's been extraordinarily successful at it, too. Many of the young couples that get married in that church come back and make it their own church home.

Author and politician Bruce Barton said, "Sometimes when I consider what tremendous consequences come from little things, I am tempted to think there are no little things."[1]

When it comes to our mission, the important thing is the willingness to embrace it. Wayne and I recently helped sponsor Race for a Soldier, a half marathon. Our son Dale who died in the year preceding the race was a runner, and it seemed a fitting way to honor his memory.

We stood at a watering station next to a milepost, and family and friends gathered to cheer on the runners. Soon Wayne and the grandkids were busy handing out water and juice to the runners as they sped past. I took my role of cheerleader seriously by applauding and shouting out encouragements.

What I found interesting was the difference between the first runners who zoomed past and the late stragglers. The serious runners barely broke stride as they grabbed the water cups, gulped down the liquid, and tossed the cups aside. Those who came later cried out, "Water. Water," as they staggered to the table and then lingered to drink it down, in no rush to continue running. I know without a doubt I would be in the latter group.

But you know what? Both groups, those athletic die-hard runners and those struggling to simply finish the course, embraced the mission to support soldiers returning from the war. And it inspired me to run my own race — to fulfill my mission — whether I finish first or struggle across the finish line long after dark.

CHRISTIAN OR SECULAR?

When we talk about our work and pleasing God with our mission, many people think that means that our work needs to be distinctively Christian. I've had criticism of my own storytelling because I write my novels for the general market, not for the Christian book market. I work to write a book that would never shame me before the Lord, whether in content or in craft. C. S. Lewis said, "What we want is not more little books about Christianity, but more little books by Christians on other subjects — with their Christianity latent."[2] That's what I try to do, allow my characters to display faith — or not — in a way that honors the story and honors God.

A fellow novelist, Susan Meissner, who writes primarily for the Christian market, wrote this:

I love Jesus and I love Story, just like the baker who loves Jesus loves bread. That doesn't etch the Gospel into every loaf he bakes, but he bakes to the glory of

148

his God and anyone who gets to know him personally will see that. He isn't selling out to bake bread a non-Christian will eat. My writing is not my ministry, it's my art form. My ministry is far bigger than my writing career. I am called to love and serve my neighbor. Writing stories is something I get to do in addition to that . . .

So whether your mission is sacred or secular doesn't matter, as long as you do it, as Eric Liddell would say, to give God pleasure.

Storytelling Prompt
What specific gifts, talents, skills, and powers have you been given for your journey through life? Why do you suppose you were gifted with these? How have you been able to use them?

The Work of Our Hands

So how do we discover the work of our hands? Frederick Buechner says, "The place God calls you to is the place where your deep gladness and the world's deep hunger meet."[3]

There are so many voices calling us to many different kinds of work — our family, including parents who may have paid for our education; our mentors; our friends; even our spouses. How do we hear God's voice in all that?

If we look at our lives we'll probably be able to find clues in our interests, passions, and skills. You should be able to find a thread that starts when you are very young and develops over time. Pay attention to those clues. They probably have God's fingerprints all over them.

Perhaps you love children, and nothing you do is as satisfying as music. Could God have called you to unlock the power and beauty of music — of worship — for children? Or what if, like me, you love to write? Does that necessarily mean you need to write for publication? Not at all. I know people who write letters to the lonely, the imprisoned, the hopeless. They change lives with their writing.

So you look for the places you've been gifted and where you are passionate. Then you look for where the need is greatest. That's the mission part. When those two things meet, you've probably found what God is calling you to do.

I'll tell you, there is no greater blessing

than to do the work for which you've been called. It is pure joy.

TEN:
AND THERE HE MET . . .

As iron sharpens iron, so one
person sharpens another.

— PROVERBS 27:17

What would a book be without characters? And what would our lives be without the people around us?

One of the interview questions I'm almost always asked is how I create the characters in my books. The question that often follows is, "Do you pattern characters after people you know?" Because my gift is that of storytelling, creating characters comes naturally to me. Story ideas are all around us; life itself presents us with plenty of ideas every single day. It's a matter of being open to them — and then fashioning them into a story with believable and compelling characters. And I think most writers find that the people around them provide the basis for the fictional characters they create. Ulti-

152

mately, believable characters come from the writer's observations about the people and situations around him or her. I never take a person from life and use him or her as a character in one of my stories. For one thing, that would be too constricting, and for another, the character needs to serve the story, not the other way around.

It comes down to observation and honesty — which is true of all characters a writer creates.

SECONDARY CHARACTERS

One of the challenging things for me as I write my books is that when I introduce a secondary character, I need to watch her carefully. Because of the way my books are so interconnected, that character may just be biding her time until she takes center stage. It's one of the reasons I try to be so mindful of each character that walks into my stories.

That's just one more way in which the stories I create are not unlike real life. How many times have we had a brief encounter with someone who later became a key player in our lives? I think of the young actor Anthony Quinn, who had a small role in the film *The Plainsman,* directed by the great Cecil B. DeMille. Quinn sensed that

Mr. DeMille held him at arm's length because of his Mexican roots. Who would have ever predicted that Cecil B. DeMille would become Anthony Quinn's father-in-law?

CHARACTERS WE DON'T WANT TO FIND IN A STORY

There are a number of characters we hope we'll not encounter when we open a book. Some of these are:

The Perfect Character

No one is ever going to pick up a book to follow the lives of perfect people living blissful existences. You'd put the book down before you'd finished the first chapter. We look for interesting characters. Flawed characters.

The Stereotypical Character

Nothing ruins a story as quickly as a stereotype. The wicked stepmother. The mad scientist. The quirky best friend. The evil landowner. It is so easy to come up with a stereotype. Because these types have been used so often in fiction, and now on the big screen and on television as well, they're the first place our minds go. A good writer has to go to the second place, the third place, or the sixty-seventh place to find a character who is unique — not a type at all.

The Cardboard Character

A cardboard character is one that's never fully fleshed out. He's as thin as cardboard, obviously propped up in the novel to meet a particular need. Sadly, we never come to know anything about him. What does he want more than anything? We feel cheated when we find a one-dimensional character in a story. I've found that some of the characters that have become my favorites start out one-dimensional and grow from there. Like Bobby Polgar in the Cedar Cove books. When we first meet him, he's a world-class chess champion and pretty much exactly as you'd expect a world-class chess champion to be, but when he meets the woman who will become his wife, he changes. He softens. At one point he confesses to Terry that with her, for the first time in his life he doesn't *think*. He *feels*.

SO WHY DO WE LOOK FOR THESE CHARACTERS TO SHOW UP IN OUR OWN STORIES?

We don't want these characters to show up in our books — they ruin the story. But these are the very people we expect to walk into our lives:

Perfect People

I confess, there have been a few days when I've wished Wayne were perfect. (I'll bet Wayne wishes I were as well.) It would be equally satisfying if all of our children were uniformly happy and satisfied, living blissful lives. And, of course, we'd prefer if the grandchildren never suffered so much as a bump in the road. I've heard so many friends wishing their lives would just "settle down." The truth is none of us are perfect. And none of us will lead perfect lives. True growth comes from overcoming problems and weathering storms.

Stereotypical People

Another confession: sometimes it's just easier to classify people by stereotypes. It's far easier to look at a mother-in-law as an interfering biddy than to look deeper and connect with her love for our spouse. It's easier to dismiss someone when we think about them as, say, street kids, rather than seeing them as God sees them and treating each one as a unique person with a history that brought him to the present. Good fiction digs deep below the surface to find the motivation and backstory, always anticipating the growth the character can make. Good life stories need to do the same.

Cardboard People

It's sad that we have to leave so many people in our lives mere cardboard outlines. When I think of the people I meet and the people who intrigue me, one of the regrets of my life is that time will not allow me to get to know them all. Our world is so interconnected that we all come across far more people than we can ever flesh out as friends. That's why I look forward to eternity. Can you imagine never having to say, "I don't have time"?

THE CHARACTERS THAT MAKE STORY COME ALIVE

If it weren't for these characters much of the story would be lost:

Villains

In most of my books I don't have villains per se — at least not the mustache-twirling, dastardly types of characters. My villains are more often the people who keep my characters from finding what they seek, one way or another. And you know, more often than not, that's the kind of antagonist you'll meet in your own life. Chances are it will not be a Simon Legree, holding the past-due mortgage over your head. It will be the supervisor who keeps passing you over for promotion simply because he never seems to see you. Or the family member who tries to subtly poison your relationships with everyone else in the family.

Without antagonists — villains — there is no story. They are the opposing force. If it were not for them, the hero would never have the opposition that leads to transformation. Guess what? It's probably the same in your life, although it may be difficult to picture an antagonist as someone God is using to help you grow. Were it not for those opposing forces, we might never break out and become all God wants us to become.

Sometimes the antagonist is not a person at all — both in fiction and in our lives. The real villain can be cancer, poverty, a string of misunderstandings, or ugly gossip. But those things can stop us dead in our tracks just as quickly as any flesh-and-blood bad guy.

Flawed Characters

Here's a secret. All good characters are flawed characters. The Bible confirms this: "As it is written: 'There is no one righteous, not even one' " (Rom. 3:10). If you expect to find anyone in your life besides wonderfully flawed characters, you will live a life of constant disappointment.

Each character I create needs to be real, which means that they are all flawed. If they were not flawed, how could they ever change and grow as the story progresses?

Walk-On Characters

These characters are fun, and sometimes unexpected. Writers often talk about having a story all planned out until an intriguing character walks onto the page. Then, without the writer ever meaning for it to happen, this new force threatens to take over the story. Sometimes it's like that in our life stories as well. Think of the number of friends who admit that when they first met their spouses, their immediate response was, "No way!" And then somehow they end up at the altar, and twenty-five years later they have a great story to tell.

That's what happened with Wayne and me. I remember when we first met. We are so different that after our first date I thought he was probably the last person I should ever marry. And yet here we are, four children and all these years later.

A few weeks ago, I had time to ponder many

of the "secondary characters" in my own life. That Sunday I flew into Washington, DC, to sign one thousand books (yes, one thousand!) at a huge warehouse in nearby Maryland for my fiction publisher, Random House. Then I ended the week in Colville, Washington, for Wayne's family reunion. I spent time with two families, my professional family — the good people in publishing — and my real-life family — my husband, my children, and a huge assortment of cousins and their children and their children's children. It brought to mind how we are all connected in one way or another. The people I met in Maryland started out as strangers when I first arrived, and I left feeling as though I had made good friends. Wayne's family is filled with aunts, uncles, cousins, fun, food, and laughter. We knew some better than others, but after a day of shared memories and deepened relationships, we left with strengthened cords of love.

If you are the hero — the protagonist — in your own story, you probably have ever-widening circles of characters in your life. You'll have close family and friends. Co-workers. Extended family. Neighbors. Acquaintances. The list of larger and larger circles could go on for a long time. All of these are the characters in your story. Some will be featured, while others may just be walk-ons.

As you continue to think about your own story, your job is the same as mine — to observe, to try to figure out why they do what they do. To love them in Jesus's name. The more you scratch the surface, the more you understand them, the richer your story will be, whether you are writing it down or just living with your eyes wide open.

Storytelling Prompt

Make a list of some of the secondary characters in your life — those unforgettable people who played smaller parts. Write or tell about one of them. How would your life have been different if you hadn't met this person?

Silence the Inner Critic

As soon as you decide to tell your own story, an unwelcome visitor shows up — the inner critic. You'll recognize his voice right away. As you start to put words on paper, it's as if he's sitting beside you. You'll write the words, "We grew up in a modest home on a nondescript street in . . . ," and immediately you'll sense him saying, "If you call it modest, you'll hurt Mom's feelings. She was so proud of that house."

Or, if you start to tell an anecdote from your childhood, he'll say, "It didn't really happen that way. You've romanticized it."

Sometimes the voice sounds like that of one of the characters in your own story. Brothers and sisters are great naysayers, and if you are telling your story you may hear them in your imagination saying, "Where in the world did you get that?" As Anne Lamott says in *Bird by Bird: Some Instructions on Writing and Life,* "You own everything that happened to you. Tell your stories. If people wanted you to write warmly about them, they should have behaved better."

As you get rolling on the story, you might look at it one day through the eyes of the inner critic and say, "This is garbage. Why did I ever think I could write this stuff?" Or maybe halfway through, you'll just decide that the story is unimportant. After all, other people have stories that are so much more interesting.

Sound familiar?

The inner critic is not just there for people who are writing their stories. If you are telling your story through scrapbook-

162

ing, you'll see someone else's world-class scrapbook and decide yours is just not up to snuff. Or if you are telling your story through photography, you'll start critiquing your technique. Why did you think you could capture life in photographs anyway?

It's important to recognize whose voice it is. It's not the voice of the Creator. We know His voice. The inner critic is the voice of the destroyer. That voice strips us of every shred of creativity God gave us.

It takes real resolve to learn to ignore that voice. Sometimes we have to do what Jesus did. In Matthew 16:21–23, He is trying to explain to His disciples what is going to happen to Him. When He predicts His death, Peter stops Him and says, "Never, Lord! This shall never happen to you!"

Jesus recognizes that even though Peter said the words, the message was actually coming from the destroyer. The Lord turns to Peter and says, "Get behind me, Satan! You are a stumbling block to me; you do not have in mind the concerns of God, but merely human concerns."

We need to say the same thing to our inner critic. "Get behind me! You are a stumbling block to me." It's important that we not let our inner critic steal the joy of telling our story.

And if your inner critic sounds like a sibling? The fear that all the characters in your story won't agree on every detail will paralyze your telling. The truth is that if each child in a family wrote the story of his or her childhood, none of the stories would look alike. Each of us sees events through his or her own filter. *Angela's Ashes* by Frank McCourt tells the story of the author's poverty-stricken upbringing in Limerick, Ireland, including his struggles with his father's drinking and his mother's attempts to feed the family. His brothers, Malachy and Alphie, both wrote memoirs about the same childhood, and each tells a distinctively different story in his own voice.

That internal voice of years of criticism and doubt can be so much louder than God's still, small voice. That's why we need to immerse ourselves in the Scriptures. We need to rewire our hearts, our souls, and our minds so that God's truth is our compass. All of us struggle with silencing the inner critic, but it's a battle we need to win in order to move past the words *once upon a time.*

Eleven:
An Old Man Sat by the
Side of the Road . . .

Therefore I am sending you prophets
and sages and teachers.
— MATTHEW 23:34A

Every good story has its mentors, its wise
women or wise men.

When I think of the wise women in my
life, my aunt Betty Stierwalt comes to mind.
As I write this, Aunt Betty, my father's
sister, will turn 102 years old next month.
You might picture a frail, bedridden existence. Not Aunt Betty. Now it's true she
uses a walker, but it doesn't stop her one
bit. That walker, which she named Walter,
takes her all over Aberdeen, South Dakota.
She's logged over seven thousand hours
through many different volunteer programs,
doing everything from peeling apples to
visiting with lonely seniors. She regularly
helps out with bingo. Her zest for life is
contagious.

When Aunt Betty was in her late nineties, my cousin and I took a trip to Aberdeen to visit her. She mentioned she'd have a tea for us. She didn't say that she planned a tea for thirty-one of her friends to meet us. That's the kind of stamina she has. She keeps up with her favorite baseball team, the Minnesota Twins, and occasionally follows football, especially the Chicago Bears, since a distant relative, Brian Urlacher, plays for the team.

Before I went in for knee replacement surgery two years ago, Aunt Betty wrote me a letter. Actually, her "sore left leg" wrote my "damaged right knee" a letter filled with encouragement and advice.

Aunt Betty is an example for those of us in the next generation, not just because she is so giving and energetic, but also because she understands what is important. Whenever anyone asks her the secret to a long life, she answers, "It's been by the grace of God. That's no secret."[1] She insists that she's going to live until she dies. That, my friends, is profound advice.

Mentors have always played an important role in my stories as well as in my life. In *The Shop on Blossom Street,* a young Alix Townsend signs up for a knitting class at A Good Yarn, the knitting shop run by Lydia

Hoffman. Alix lives with a roommate in a rundown apartment, since she has no family to speak of — her mother's in prison for check forgery and her father is, well, who knows where. Her lost soul of a roommate had slipped a small stash of marijuana in Alix's purse to avoid violating parole, and Alix had been caught with it. Rather than try to explain and get her roommate into even deeper trouble, Alix shouldered the blame and had been assigned community service. With some serious misgivings, she decides to knit a baby blanket to be given away as part of that community service and begins to attend the class.

The group that gathers in the shop for this knitting class couldn't be more diverse. The shop owner, Lydia, opened the shop as she was recovering from cancer — she knew she needed a healing place, and knitting was her passion. Jacqueline Donovan is a socialite, married to the architect who spearheaded the renovation and gentrification of Blossom Street. And Carol Girard is knitting a blanket as she and her husband continue frustrating infertility treatments. An unlikely group for sure, but as the story develops, the women become friends and Alix finds the wise women — the mentors — she has longed for in her life.

IDENTIFYING OUR MENTORS

I'm guessing that in the story of your life you've had a number of mentors. Some may have been family — mothers, aunts, grandmothers. Others may have been teachers, professors, or people from your church. Some of you may have found mentors among your colleagues or your bosses.

One of the most interesting questions you can ask is, who mentored you? Oprah Winfrey talks about her fourth-grade teacher, Mrs. Duncan, who showed her it was okay to be smart. Mrs. Duncan encouraged her love of reading and set her on a path to success. Oprah wrote, "A mentor is someone who allows you to see the hope inside yourself. A mentor is someone who allows you to know that no matter how dark the night, in the morning joy will come. A mentor is someone who allows you to see the higher part of yourself when sometimes it becomes hidden to your own view."[2]

When we are telling our own stories, an important step is to identify our mentors. I could name so many, like the people I know personally — my parents, my family members, my first librarian, my pastors, and my Bible study leaders, as well as those who've mentored me in publishing. But I can also name those who mentored me through their books, like Dr. Norman Vincent Peale, Zig Ziglar, John Maxwell, and others who've written the hundreds of business or motivational books I've read over the years.

Other mentors have been the novelists I've read and admired through the years. These talented writers have helped me hone my style just by reading their writing. I've learned valuable lessons from their skills.

It's an important exercise to remember all those who lead the way in our lives. Wouldn't it be fun to create a book of mentors? Forget the high school yearbook, how about a yearbook of the mentor-like characters that have been part of our lives, complete with photos and quotes?

MENTORING OTHERS

Having mentors is important, but so is being a mentor. We want to be that wise old man or wise old woman, no matter what age we are. It's a two-way street. In his book *The Mentor Leader: Secrets to Building People and Teams That Win Consistently,* coach Tony Dungy says, "Remember that mentor leadership is all about serving. Jesus said, 'For even the Son of Man came not to be served but to serve others and to give his life as a ransom for many' " (Mark 10:45).[3]

Whether intentionally or unintentionally,

we are teaching and modeling for others. We will be written into many a story. It shouldn't surprise us that family members, especially children and grandchildren, see us as mentors. "Things my mama taught me" is a strong theme in people's life stories.

I think we would be surprised (and maybe humbled) to discover all the people who might consider us part of their life stories.

THE BEST EXAMPLE

Jesus set a perfect example for mentorship when He chose His twelve disciples. He regularly spoke to thousands of people, but He knew that He needed to train a handful of men to follow in His footsteps. This was more than a figure of speech. He selected twelve men who literally followed him, footstep by footstep, as he taught and healed, ate and prayed, slept and traveled.

He mentored them systematically and, in the Scriptures, explained the reason behind each step. Some of the specifics of His mentoring were:

- **He taught.** The disciples not only caught His teaching as He taught great crowds on the hillsides and in the temple, but also learned from Him individually and as a group over meals and in quiet moments. "A student is not above his teacher, but everyone who is fully trained will be like his teacher" (Luke 6:40).

- **He modeled.** So much of mentoring takes place when the disciples passively observe the mentor. Jesus's disciple, Peter, wrote, "His divine power has given us everything we need for life and godliness through our knowledge of Him" (2 Pet. 1:3).

- **He asked questions.** We call this the Socratic method of teaching — asking questions rather than just imparting knowledge. It allows the student to develop his own answers, to seek the information, to form his own opinion. This is how Jesus taught. "But what about you?" he asked. "Who do you say I am?" (Matt. 16:15).

- **He believed.** By all accounts this was a ragtag bunch of men, for the most part. One was a doctor, another a much-despised tax collector, and several were fishermen, but Jesus believed in them. He saw more in them than they saw in themselves. If we were to choose twelve people to change the world, we'd probably pore over résumés and agonize over background checks and past experience. Jesus looked at these men and saw their hearts. He saw potential, not the past or the present. "Follow Me and I will make you fishers of men" (Matt. 4:19).

- **He developed.** Jesus patiently helped His disciples develop character. As we read the Gospels we can trace the growth of these men — the ups and downs — as they built the traits they needed to do the job set before them. "We can participate in His divine nature through faith, goodness, knowledge, self-control, perseverance, godliness, brotherly kindness, and love" (2 Pet. 1:4–7).

- **He empowered.** In corporate mentorship programs, this is often the most difficult aspect of mentoring — allowing the mentee to fly on his own. For many mentors, this is threatening. What if the mentee flies higher than his teacher? Jesus knew he was preparing his disciples to follow in his footsteps and not only empowered them with knowledge but sent them the ultimate empowerment, the Holy Spirit. He inspired them and equipped them to go out and change the world. "As the Father has sent me, so send I you" (John 20:21).

- **He loved.** Love is the key to a good mentor. Jesus loved these disciples. "Love one another as I have loved you. By this will all men know that you are my disciples" (John 13:34–35).

Time slips by so quickly; we need to take every opportunity to capture the lives of the characters that have been the wise old women and wise old men in our own stories.

Storytelling Prompt
Who have been the mentors — the wise old women and wise old men — in your life? What have you learned from them? How have they changed you?

Alternative: Name one of your mentors and explain how his or her influence changed the direction of your life.

Capturing Wisdom

Alex Haley, author of *Roots,* is one of the writers whose autograph is featured in my collection. He once said, "Every time an old person dies it's as though a library has burned." I've thought of that so often since the passing of my mother and father. How I wish I could go back and ask more questions. I find myself wishing I had written more down, remembered more.

You may still have some of your elders and some of the mentors in your life. While there is still time, be intentional about recording their stories. Don't rely on your memory. My friend had an aunt in her nineties who remembered the tiniest details about her life from the time she wore diapers to the present. She observed the world around her with a keen eye. When she began recalling something that happened in their family or in their town, my friend would pull out paper and pencil and jot things down. Now that her aunt is gone, my friend says she's so glad to have those notes, since her own memory doesn't hold a candle to her aunt's.

Another friend, Dietrich Nelson, told me the story of his grandmother. She crossed the plains in a covered wagon as an infant, held in her mother's arms. Yet before she died in the 1960s, she flew in a jet plane. Just think of the stories she had to tell.

During the Great Depression, early in 1930s, the government initiated the Federal Writers' Project, sending interviewers all across the South to record the stories of former slaves. They used primitive recording devices, but those slave testimonies were preserved.

A century-old church wanted to capture some of the memories of days long gone. They knew that many of their oldest members would be too self-conscious to sit in a chair and speak directly to a video camera, so they planned a series of dessert get-togethers where the old friends sat around a table, coffee cups in hand, and shared stories on a single subject at a time. One night might cover transportation, leading to discussions of the horse-drawn school bus and the driver who would always bring homemade cookies on Fridays for an after-school snack. The discussions would meander down fascinating rabbit trails, but those holding the cameras did a wonderful job of being unobtrusive and still capturing the wisdom and living history firsthand.

TWELVE:
THE UNSEEN WORLD
GATHERED . . .

So we fix our eyes not on what is seen,
but on what is unseen, since
what is seen is temporary,
but what is unseen is eternal.
— 2 CORINTHIANS 4:18

On Thanksgiving, my family usually takes time to go around the dining room table and recount the blessing for which we are most grateful. One Thanksgiving a few years ago, however, we did something a little different. I asked each member of my family to tell about the time when they felt God's presence most distinctly. We went around the table, and the stories were wonderful — rich and revealing. Then it was my dad's turn. Dad never liked to talk about his World War II experiences. In fact, I didn't learn that my father had been a POW in Germany until my own son was in the military. Dad never spoke of his experiences until he was in his late seventies. So when he started talking about feeling God's presence, we were all surprised at the story he told.

He landed on the beach at Normandy six days after the first landing on D-day. He said he remembered it like it was yesterday. As the troop carrier jockeyed into position for the landing, the sound of artillery shelling was almost as loud as the beating of his heart. The smell of smoke and death hung over the beach, but there was no time to contemplate what was coming. Wave after wave, the troops stepped into the water to make their way toward the beach. Dad carried his gear in a pack strapped to his back. As he told us the story that day, he said it was a fifty-pound pack. I've since read that the packs were actually nearly a hundred pounds of dry weight. Of course, they weren't dry for long. Water weighs more than eight pounds per gallon. It's estimated that as soon as those packs got wet, they weighed upward of three hundred pounds. The water was six or seven feet deep, but most of the men somehow managed to keep their heads above water as they made for the beach. Dad, however, sank like a rock to the bottom. The water was murky from all the activity, but he said he would never forget the chilling sight of the hundreds of drowned men, weighted down by their heavy gear. Short men, he added. My dad topped out at barely five foot five. With the weight of his pack, there was no way he could fight his way to the surface. He was drowning, pushed this way and that by the press of soldiers fighting their way toward the beach. He knew he would soon be taking his place among the casualties buried in that watery mass grave. The last thing he remembered was surrendering his spirit to God.

Dad woke up amid the noise and confusion on the beach. He had no idea how he'd gotten there. It could be that he had been dragged up out of the water by a strong soldier and left on the beach to fend for himself, but I don't think he believed that. That Thanksgiving Day, he lowered his voice to something barely above a whisper and said it could very well have been the hand of an angel. As with most unseen things, we will never know for sure. Yet my father remembered that day as a profound turning point in his life — the day he knew God watched over him and chose life for him.

FACT OR FANTASY?

The unseen world plays an important part in our stories. Too often, we feel the need to stick to the facts, but facts are only a part of our story. There is the temporal world, for sure. That is the world we see and hear and taste and smell and feel. It is soil sifting through our fingers and children hugging our necks. But the entire time we are walking through the terra firma of our lives, unseen things are swirling around us.

A story I told in my book *God's Guest List* comes to mind. In the last years of his life, my dad hated having to use a walker, especially in his own home. But he never lost his independent spirit, even though he lost his ability to walk steadily. One night Dad got up out of his bed in the middle of the night to use the restroom. He took off without his walker. He got to the hallway and sagged against the wall because he wasn't strong enough to get himself back to the bedroom.

He was stuck there, leaning against the wall, when out of nowhere a man in overalls showed up. My dad described him in great detail, saying he was dressed like a farmer. Because Dad was in a desperate situation, he didn't bother to question the farmer. He knew he had to get back to bed before he collapsed, and so my ever-practical father said, "Hey buddy, I could sure use some help here."

The man didn't say anything, but he gently helped my dad back to bed, stood over him for a moment, and then, as mysteriously as he had appeared, he vanished.

My dad was a great storyteller, but he never confused fact and fiction, even to the day he died. He was simply grateful that the man helped him to bed.

This incident reminds me of the verse in Acts 27:23 (KJV), "For there stood by me this night the angel of God, whose I am, and whom I serve."

CONFLICTED REACTIONS

Have you ever noticed that when we talk about the unseen things, we often get two distinctly different reactions? Some people relish angel stories and stories of the Lord's direct intervention in our lives. They can't seem to get enough of them. The other group consists of those materialists — the I-have-to-see-it-to-believe-it fraternity — who fold arms over chests and smirk at the emotionalism of the first group. And if you add any talk about the unseen evil things, well . . .

Here's the truth:

180

- Angels do exist and do intervene in our lives. You need only read the Bible to see that. They are mentioned some 108 times in the Old Testament and 165 times in the New Testament.
- Angels are not some form of human beings. They existed long before God created us. This means that when we die, we don't become angels. Many people say things at funerals like, "There's a new angel in heaven today," but that is just a way of acknowledging that their loved one is with Jesus.
- The primary job of angels is to worship God in heaven. We also see them delivering messages, like the visits to Mary and to Joseph announcing that Jesus would be born. They guide us, as they did Cornelius in Acts 10. They sometimes provide for physical needs, like they did for Christ in Matthew 4:11. They protect us. This is the job we most often think of — guardian angels. The Bible often talks about the angels keeping watch over us. Sometimes they get us out of trouble, as they did for Peter in Acts 12. And, in death, they care for us and escort us into eternity, just as they did for Lazarus in Luke 16:22.

- Angels are nothing like the cherubic, rosy-cheeked infants we often see in paintings or as images affixed to modern-day giftware. They are spirits, though we know they can take the form of human-like bodies. Hebrews 13:2 implies this when it says, "Do not forget to show hospitality to strangers, for by so doing some people have shown hospitality to angels without knowing it." Many times we read about them in frightening terms — like lightning, and with garments whiter and more dazzling than anything known in our world. And when angels make appearances, they generally appear in the form of men.

THE SEEN AND UNSEEN

One of my favorite things to do is to include the unseen world in my stories. If you've read my fiction you probably know three of my readers' favorite characters are the angels Shirley, Goodness, and Mercy. Three angels who protect, guide, and, well, intrude on the lives of mere mortals. Are they theologically correct? Of course not — it's fiction. Storytelling. Nowhere in the Bible do we see female-seeming angels (though who's to say they couldn't take on that form?). And nowhere in the Bible do we see the trouble sometimes caused by these three. But I've enjoyed writing the angel books because they demonstrate, in a fun way, that God cares about our lives and intervenes. As a nod to authenticity, I'm adding a male angel in the next book, *Angels at the Table.* Why add another angel, you ask? It just seemed like a fun addition to the trio. And because the names Shirley, Goodness, and Mercy are adaptations from verse 6 of the beloved twenty-third psalm, the new angel's name is Will. (Surely goodness and mercy *will* follow you . . .)

A GLIMPSE INTO THE UNSEEN WORLD

Every now and then we get a glimpse into the unseen world. Skeptics doubt the near-death experiences that get reported, but surely there are too many of these stories, with too many similarities, to be discounted wholesale.

Those who care for the dying say that at the end of life, the dividing line between the known world and the unseen world becomes very thin. Some call it the "Thin Places." Don't you love that description? Research shows that when they are nearing death, people often seem to begin an organic process of confronting unfinished issues. It's not unusual in the days or weeks before death for the dying person to report being visited by long-gone relatives, friends, or other people. Often the purpose of these visits as reported is to help the dying person "let go." Others report going on journeys to otherworldly realms, or the caretakers will see them stare at a certain point in the room and then break into a look of sheer amazement. My mother was with her sister Paula when she died, and just seconds before she passed from life to death, my aunt Paula's eyes widened with sheer wonder, as if she had caught a glimpse of the new life that awaited her in heaven.

DOES THIS MEAN WE ALL GO TO HEAVEN?

Many Christians discount these stories because the moment of eternity — of seeing the great light — seems to indiscriminately come to those who are followers of Jesus as well as to those who've rejected Him. That does not seem to track with what popular culture teaches. We've all seem cinematographic images of some people whisked away to heaven and others, like in the movie *Ghost,* being sucked into hell.

It's true that not everyone will go to

heaven. We know from reading the Bible that the Lord does not push the kingdom of heaven onto anyone. It's a matter of free will, and we do have to act upon the invitation in order to spend eternity in heaven. But we also know that eternity *is* for everyone, whether we choose heaven or not. We will all live forever in the unseen realms. And when we die, we will all see heaven, because we will stand before the throne of judgment.

GLIMPSES OF ETERNITY

In the book *The Art of Dying,* authors Peter and Elizabeth Fenwick relate the following: "The male patient asked us to stand one on each side of him because he wanted to thank us for looking after him. He then looked over my shoulder towards the window and said, 'Hang on, I will be with you in a minute, I just want to thank these nurses for looking after me.' The patient repeated himself a couple of times, then he died."[1]

Thomas Edison's last words, as he emerged briefly from a coma, were, "It is very beautiful over there." And legend has it that as he was dying, Beethoven said, "I shall hear in heaven!"

My favorite story just happened in the fall

of last year, when Steve Jobs, the founder of Apple, died. According to his biographer, Walter Isaacson, in his last few interviews with Steve Jobs, this man who created beauty out of technology had become increasingly interested in God and life after death. In a striking eulogy written by his sister, Mona Simpson, she tells about his last hours, how he gathered his beloved family around him as he slowly slipped away. Before embarking on his final journey, she said, he looked for a long time at his wife, then at each of his children. Then he looked past them, over their shoulders, and said, "Oh wow. Oh wow. Oh wow."[2]

The unseen world. It's part of the stories I tell and it is part of your own story as well, if only you will have eyes to see. "Yet the LORD hath not given you a heart to perceive, and eyes to see, and ears to hear, unto this day" (Deut. 29:4 KJV).

We need to be willing to squint into the sunlight and catch glimmers of mystery and wonder. And when we are telling our own stories we need not shy away from the miracles.

Storytelling Prompt

Are you ever aware of the unseen world around you? Does God seem real to you or are you just catching glimmers of Him? Do you have God incidents to add to your story?

Catching Glimmers

In our modern world, we practically worship science. We expect the world to be explained, cataloged, and viewed in concrete terms. Black-and-white terms. Legal analysts tell us that these days it is more difficult than ever to get a conviction based on circumstantial evidence. Juries have watched far too many episodes of *CSI* and expect concrete evidence — DNA, surveillance tapes, blood spatter analysis. Solid proof. There's no room for nonscientific evidence.

G. K. Chesterton, the much-acclaimed twentieth-century British writer, spent many years exploring the clash of science and religion. He concluded that though those who avidly practiced science — the materialists — were entirely logical in their strict belief system, in which they explained everything with natural events, the fact that they couldn't allow for the pos-

187

sibility of the tiniest miracle locked them into a disbelief that would not allow for exploration and observation. He wrote that orthodox Christians were freer because they could believe in both natural and supernatural causes for events.

Too many people try to take our stories and apply the same standard of science and logic, but in our hearts, we know there is more. We long to catch glimmers of the divine in our books as well as in the stories of our lives. As I write my books, I want the stories to be logical, but at the same time I hope to capture a bit of the divine — just like in real life.

THIRTEEN:
TROUBLE WAS BOUND TO
COME . . .

I have told you these things,
so that in me you may have peace.
In this world you will have trouble.
But take heart!
I have overcome the world.

— JOHN 16:33

Remember the 1957 Meredith Willson musical *The Music Man*? One of the more popular songs sung by Professor Harold Hill was "Ya Got Trouble." That trouble in River City was the centerpiece of the plot. Had the professor not convinced the good citizens that they had trouble that needed to be addressed, trouble that would lead their youngsters down the slippery slope to ruin, none of the townspeople would have been interested in purchasing musical instruments for their children.

Character grows when there is conflict. Plot grows out of trouble. No conflict? No

189

story. It's true when I write stories, but it's just as true in our own lives.

Trouble. It's something we generally want to avoid at all costs. But the truth is that trouble is our lot in life. Chris Tiegreen, in his book *The One Year Walk with God Devotional,* quotes Warren Wiersbe as saying, "The Christian life is not a playground; it is a battleground."[1]

DEVELOPING CONFLICT

In my novels, one of the most important things I must do is develop conflict. To do this, I look at my characters and figure out two things: their deepest longings and their biggest fears. In chapter 11, I talked about the plot for my book *The Shop on Blossom Street.* The characters in the knitting class all have stories and conflicts that give rise to trouble. Remember the young Alix Townsend, who took the rap for the drugs her roommate hid in her purse? Her deepest longing is to have a "normal" life like the other ladies in her knitting class. She's afraid of drugs, having seen how they devastated her family. Coming into contact with drugs again was her biggest fear. So bearing the false accusation of drug possession sets her up for conflict. It plays on her worst fears and puts her longing — to be accepted by "normal" people — even farther out of reach.

Jacqueline Donovan is a socialite who's spent years dreaming of the perfect life and the perfect wife for her only son, Paul. Her greatest fear is somehow losing him. So when he falls in love with the down-home Tammie Lee, a Southern girl from the wrong side of the tracks, conflict is inevitable.

The third person in the class, Carol Girard, longs for a child. After trying unsuccessfully for so long, her greatest fear is that she won't be able to get pregnant. As she begins to knit her baby blanket we sense her intense baby hunger.

Three women who long for something they don't have and whose greatest fears seem to be coming true. It's the perfect setup for a story. Conflict builds characters and characters build conflict.

Life is not unlike fiction. In fact, soon after I wrote about Carol's inability to conceive, my son Dale and his wife, Laurie, began that same journey to overcome infertility. It was a long, frustrating road, with six IVF attempts. Every time we cuddle the now-two-year-old Jaxon, we are reminded that good things — precious things — come out of trouble.

OPPORTUNITY GROWS OUT OF TROUBLE

Someone once told me that the Chinese word for crisis consists of two characters — the one for danger and the one for opportunity. That makes sense, doesn't it?

We long for a calm life. How often have you wished everything would "settle down"? I have many a friend who's expressed a longing for quiet and uneventful family gatherings at Christmas or other holidays. As one of my friends says, "My extended family puts the fun in dysfunctional." But you can bet that her family is ever changing, hopefully growing stronger and closer as they meet each challenge and recommit to each other. Where there is potential conflict, there is potential for great growth. It's an opportunity. Exciting challenges do not grow out of a calm existence.

TO BE REDEEMED

In his book *Soulprint,* Mark Batterson says, "Trouble ought to come with a footnote in fine print, 'to be redeemed.' "[2] He talks about how the longer he lives, the more he has come to see that disappointments in life are often divine appointments. Trouble may just be a delay in all that the Lord has for us.

192

I'm beginning to believe I'm an expert on trouble. Earlier this year, after suffering the greatest loss of my life when we buried our son Dale, I underwent what should have been a simple surgery and ended up with complications that landed me in the intensive care unit for seven days. I was home only a few days before Wayne fell, breaking his arm in two places and tearing his rotator cuff, which required surgery. It felt as though things could not have gotten much worse, but that was before I came down with a severe case of shingles. In my pain and frustration I complained to God that I was beginning to feel like Job of the Old Testament. No sooner had I uttered the words than I seemed to hear the Lord saying to me, "But Debbie, don't lose sight of the blessings that followed." I grabbed my Bible and there it was. In Job 42:10 it says, "After Job had prayed for his friends, the LORD restored his fortunes and gave him twice as much as he had before." Skipping down to verse 12, it says, "The LORD blessed the latter part of Job's life more than the former part." I knew then that the Lord would bless me . . . that He already had blessed me.

RAISING THE STAKES

To keep a story moving forward, sometimes the author has to raise the stakes. This device reminds me of the movie *Speed.* When a terrorist's plan backfires, he rigs a ticking time bomb to a Los Angeles city bus. The bus must maintain a speed of at least fifty miles per hour to keep from exploding. Anyone who knows LA traffic, with its congestion and twists and turns, understands what an impossible task the terrorist has set for the hero. To further complicate things, if the LAPD tries to unload any passengers, the bomb will be detonated remotely. At each turn the stakes are higher until we are on the edges of our seats, pulling for the good guys.

In our own stories we often see the stakes being raised as well. Haven't there been times in your life when you felt as if you couldn't bear one more thing? And what happens? One more thing. As we see the stakes being raised, we need to recognize God's hand at work. Danger plus opportunity.

INTERNAL COMPLICATIONS

I know you've heard the words, "Well, she brought that on herself." There's no question that sometimes we complicate our own

194

lives. There are people who are nothing short of chaos makers. If their lives are too smooth they'll stir something up. These chaos makers can be great characters in a book, though not so much in our lives.

But internal complications are a fact of life. You may have things that happened to you as a child that will forever impact your life. Those internal complications will shade your dealings with other people and will even color the way you see the world. Danger plus opportunity. Until you embrace the opportunity to deal with the complication — to take it before the Lord or to work it out in counseling — it will spell trouble for you.

EXTERNAL COMPLICATIONS

Internal complications — sometimes even trouble of our own making — are one thing, but what about those troubles that come to us through no fault of our own? I'll never forget those years, early in our marriage, when our children were young, and we discovered that the land on which our house stood was toxic. Homes were vacated. Other families in our neighborhood were uprooted. When we had purchased our home we'd had no inkling of the trouble that lay just below the surface. Something had to be done. Eventually the city of Seattle made good and stepped forward to buy the homes, but there were many battles to be fought before that war was won.

I also think about my friend Carol Kent, whose life changed forever when her twenty-five-year-old son, a graduate of the U.S. Naval Academy and a lieutenant in the navy with an impeccable military record, shot and killed his wife's ex-husband, believing he was protecting his two stepdaughters from the risk of abuse. Her son — her only son — received a sentence of life in prison in Florida with no possibility of parole. Carol tells her story in her books *When I Lay My Isaac Down* and *A New Kind of Normal*.

Carol Kent knows trouble, but here's what she says:

I've learned that God is close to the brokenhearted and He never wastes our sorrow. I'm continuing to experience a new kind of normal where I can make hope-filled choices based on His eternal truth. Every day I try to find one thing to be thankful for and it's my goal to look around and do one tangible act of loving compassion for someone else who is walking a difficult path. I'm also learn-

ing that God gives us splashes of joy —
and even laughter — in the middle of a
difficult journey.[3]

DEEPENING THE STORY

Writers often speak about deepening the
story. This is done by introducing complications that grow out of a rich inner life.
That's a great goal for us as we live our lives
and tell our stories. In order to rise to the
challenge of trouble, we need to feed our
inner lives. We read in the first chapter
about the importance of listening to our
lives and Socrates' contention that "the unexamined life is not worth living."

We will overcome trouble as we deepen
our relationship with the Lord. And how do
we deepen our relationship? The same way
we do with our spouses, our friends, or our
children. We spend quality time together.

God tells us that in this world we will have
trouble. It's a given. What we do with those
challenges is entirely up to us. Remember,
without a crucifixion there would be no
resurrection.

Storytelling Prompt
Describe a time when trouble knocked at
your door. Looking back, do you see any
redemption? Try to re-create a troubled or

tense scene that you've never forgotten through the eyes of your child-self. Did you ever have a season when trouble just began piling up — one thing after another until you could hardly see your way out? What did it feel like when you were in the middle of that?

Imagination

When trouble comes, is it ever half as bad as we had imagined it? We often hear someone say a variation on the following: "I wish I could just get this awful thing over with. Imagining the outcome is killing me."

One of the skills we need to master in life is the management of our imagination. On one hand, we need to let it run free. It's a powerful thing when used creatively. When we imagine what we can be or what we can accomplish, it becomes a great motivator. But when we dwell on the negative and spend our energy imagining the worst-case scenarios of our lives, imagination will defeat us.

We know about worst-case-scenario thinking. That's when we imagine things all out of proportion. It's the high school senior facing finals who imagines failure on the test leading to not receiving enough credits to graduate, leading to having to earn a GED instead of getting a diploma, leading to giving up his seat at the college that already accepted him, leading to . . . well, you can see how far imagination can take us if directed toward the negative. We can be so creative when imagining imminent doom. And you know what? It paralyzes us. It becomes self-fulfilling prophecy.

Second Corinthians 10:5 holds the answer for us. "We demolish arguments and every pretension that sets itself up against the knowledge of God, and we take captive every thought to make it obedient to Christ." We *take captive every thought.*

In other words, we need to keep from what many call "stinkin' thinkin'."

My friend's grandmother wanted to learn to drive in the early days of automobiles. Not many women drove at that time, but she was determined. Her husband took her out to a smooth field, flat and open for as far as the eye could see. The only obstacle in the whole acreage was a lone tree. Her husband settled her behind the wheel of that shiny black Model T Ford, showed her how everything worked, and, as he climbed into the passenger seat, joked, "Now just don't hit the tree, Ruth."

Well, you can guess what happened, right? Acres and acres of open space and she headed right for that tree. She focused on the tree — on the one obstacle — and she hit it smack dab in the middle of the bumper. She never did learn to drive, though she tried it several times through the years. She used to say, "Give me a tree, no matter how distant, and I'll manage to hit it." Self-fulfilling prophecy. If we can imagine it, we can attain it. Unfortunately that works both for us and against us.

In his book *Soulprint,* Mark Batterson talks about Leonardo da Vinci and the two distinct kinds of imagining he wrote about: preimagining and postimagining. We know all about preimagining. That's the imagination we usually refer to. It's imagining what something will be like before it even happens. Postimagining is reimagining the past — those things that have already come to pass.

Batterson says that our ability to post-imagine — to put things into perspective once some time has passed — will determine how well we live life. I agree. I often write about characters who have allowed the troubles of their pasts to embitter them. They are not free to love again, to live fully, or to see people through God's eyes.

So while it's important for us to imagine creatively in order to reach for God's best, we also need to postimagine — to see God's hand in our lives.

One of my friends struggled with infertility and, after years of trying, found herself pregnant. She and her husband were overjoyed and savored every moment of the pregnancy. When the time came for her to give birth, one complication after another arose, and their baby boy died a few hours later. It's hard to imagine more of a worst-case scenario, but through a series of miracles my friend was able to adopt a baby just a few months later. As she postimagines the events, she says that she can't imagine it any other way. Though she still mourns the little boy, she sees that had it not been for his passing, she would never have the daughter who was always meant to be theirs. No bitterness, just seeing God's hand in unimaginable circumstances.

When it comes to trouble — and we know trouble will always find us — we need to minimize worst-case-scenario thinking and put our energy into postimagining in order to see how the trouble was instrumental in shaping us.

FOURTEEN:
AND THE CHALLENGE OF HIS LIFE LOOMED . . .

God is our refuge and strength,
an ever-present help in trouble.
Therefore we will not fear, though the
earth give way and the mountains fall
into the heart of the sea, though its
waters roar and foam and the mountains
quake with their surging.
— PSALM 46:1–3

In my books I often create that moment when it looks like all will be lost. When we talk about the classic hero's journey, this is the ordeal stage. It's when the hero faces his greatest fear, often called the deepest, darkest cave. In the last chapter we talked about troubles. We all have them and they come at us with great frequency. This is different. This is the event that marks a change in our lives forever.

The year 2011 was that time for me. I woke early on Easter Sunday, as I did most mornings. I was the only one awake as I reached for my Bible. The scent of spring was in the air even before the sun rose. I savored this time I spend each day with the Lord. Wayne and I would be joining our children and grandchildren later for church services, followed by a big family breakfast.

I had already wrapped a gift for each of my children. It was a book I'd recently read about heaven. The story involved the near-death experience of a four-year-old and his incredible telling of what life was like in the great beyond. The book had fascinated and encouraged me, and I felt it was the perfect Easter gift for them.

FACING THE ABYSS

Opening my Bible, I smiled at the rising sun and thought about the brokenhearted Mary Magdalene and the other women walking to Christ's tomb that early morn. As I read the familiar verses I realized anew the terrible price Jesus had paid for my passage into heaven. I bowed my head and closed my eyes, and as I did I had a vision. The image was that of a tunnel, dark and bleak, with a bright light shining at the end. It was like the one I'd read about so often in writings by those who have stood on the precipice of death. In that moment I realized that it was Jesus who carved that tunnel. He died; He descended and was there for three days. I often wondered what had happened during that time. All the Bible says is that He descended. In that moment I understood. Jesus had freed the multitude of souls who had been awaiting His arrival. The saints who had passed: Moses, Samuel, David, Daniel, and literally thousands of others who had been His faithful servants. They needed to wait for Jesus to carve that tunnel. I don't often have such visions, and this one excited and encouraged me. I woke my husband and later told my children about this beautiful vision God had given me of the saints walking joyously toward the light, following their Redeemer.

Little did I know that just four months later, Wayne and I would stand brokenhearted over our son's grave. My solace was the knowledge that this was the very tunnel Jesus had carved out by His death and resurrection. Jesus was there to greet our son on the other side.

THE DARKNESS GATHERS

Our son Dale suffered from depression, and recently his life had been beset with difficulties. He was on medication, but a recent DUI ticket and what that would mean to his teaching career further complicated his perspective on life. I realized that for our son this was as much a spiritual battle as a physical one. Every morning, I faithfully brought Dale before the Lord. I'd told Satan he couldn't have my son and I was prepared to do battle — and I meant it.

I couldn't forget that three years earlier, Dale had gone to the Holy Land with a pastor friend of ours and was baptized in the Sea of Galilee. He joked with me and said, "Gee, Mom, all you had to do was send the other kids to Bible camp. Me, you had to send all the way to Israel." For a long time afterward, he was on the right path, and then all of a sudden everything seemed to go awry.

One week before Dale went missing, I sat praying for him, as I did every morning, when a dark, oppressive spirit came over me. Words fail as I try to describe this heavy darkness that descended on me. For a moment I could barely breathe, and then I broke into sobs. When my husband asked me what had happened, I said, "Something's wrong with Dale. I can feel it. We're losing our son."

I called and talked to Dale later that day, and he assured me all was well. It wasn't. I believe now that was the day our son decided to take his own life.

WHEN ALL SEEMS LOST

A week later, Dale turned up missing. He'd sent vague text messages telling each of his family members of his love. I was busy with a business meeting and perturbed that he would pull one of his stunts when it was inconvenient and embarrassing. His wife was in a panic and so were his siblings. I, on the other hand, was convinced Dale had either entered rehab or had run away, something he'd done before. It would be just like him to think he could escape his troubles.

I didn't take the fact he'd been missing for twenty-four hours seriously until his wife contacted Search and Rescue. Dale's car was found, and the family gathered together and prayed as bloodhounds searched the area. They found nothing. I was the optimist, reassuring the others. Dale would be found alive and well. He just needed to get away and think things through.

Our elder son, Ted, spent the night with Wayne and me. The next morning I rose and reached for my Bible. The verse for that day was John 6:39. It read, "And this is the will of him who sent me, that I shall lose none of all those he has given me, but raise them up at the last day." In that moment I knew, as only a mother can, that our son was dead. Ted found me sobbing and reminded me I was the one who gave everyone confidence. "Don't lose faith now, Mom," he urged. But in my heart I knew Dale was gone. As Ted left I reached for the phone and called our two daughters, asking them to come to the house right away.

Instead of heading directly home, as he had intended, Ted stopped off at the area where the bloodhounds had searched only a short while before. In the woods he found evidence that his brother was close by. He contacted the sheriff's department and together they located Dale's body.

The leader of the Search and Rescue group told us that in thirty-one years of experience he's never had his dogs be that close to a body and not find it. In retrospect, I understand that God didn't want a dog to find our son, and so He sent Dale's best friend — his older brother. Nor did God wish for a stranger to come to relay the news to our family that our son had committed suicide. My daughters and husband were with me when Ted contacted us with the devastating news. God had placed His loving arms around us and given us the gracious cushion of His love.

The Lord was so very present on the worst day of my life.

A VERY PRESENT HELP

Dale's funeral was packed with family, friends, and his former students. The church was filled to overflowing. We placed his high school letterman's jacket in the front of the church, along with his favorite pair of running shoes. His brother gave his eulogy and his two sisters worked on the photo display in the church vestibule, along with a video set to his favorite karaoke song, "You're So Vain." Ted set up a Facebook page titled "Remembering Dale Macomber" and literally hundreds of entries were posted within a few days. A sense of unreality settled over me as we celebrated the life of our son.

Following the reception, just the family went to the cemetery. I'd been emotionally strong through the funeral and the reception, but when we reached the graveyard and I viewed my son's casket being lowered into the ground, it felt as if someone had thrust a knife into my heart. Grief overwhelmed me and I broke into sobs. How could this have happened? Why would our son, who was always so loving and tender, bring such horrific pain into our lives? None of this made sense. None of this felt real.

As we got ready to leave, my husband came to me and Dale's wife, Laurie. He placed his arms around each of us and steered us toward Jody, our elder daughter. "I want you to take your mother and Laurie home," he said.

I looked up at him in disbelief. I couldn't understand why Wayne wouldn't want to return home with us. If ever there was a time I needed my husband, it was then. How could he even think of leaving me at such a time?

"What are you going to do?" I asked.

My husband looked at me, and with tears in his eyes, he said, "I'm not going to let a stranger with a backhoe bury our son. I'm going to do it myself."

Ted stayed with his father, and together the two of them buried Dale. Wayne and I have been married more than forty years, and in all those years, I have never loved my husband more than at that moment.

As you tell your story, you'll recognize your own deepest, darkest cave. It's only in telling the story that we begin to see God's hand. I've learned that it isn't until you are facing your own black tunnel — the biggest challenge of your life — that God reveals how He's been preparing you for this.

Storytelling Prompt

Have you had a deepest, darkest cave experience in your life? Try to recapture your emotions during the ordeal. Tell about it without the benefit of hindsight, without the redemption that may have come since.

Dark Night of the Soul

As you live your story you may find times when it feels as if God is nowhere to be found. John of the Cross, a Carmelite monk who lived in sixteenth-century Castile, wrote about this in his poem "The Dark Night of the Soul" and later writings. He suffered that dark night and realized that it was part of the spiritual journey. He sensed that God wanted to take him deeper, and in order to do that he needed to be weaned off the emotional and taken deeper into obedience and an understanding of his failings.

There have been times in my own spiritual story when the Lord seemed especially quiet. There were times when I prayed fervently and could not sense an answer, times when I wondered, "Where is God in all this?"

Agnes Gonxha Bojaxhiu, born in Albania, is better known to us as Mother Teresa of

210

Calcutta — winner of a Nobel Prize, selfless servant to the poor and dying in India, and an example of obedient service to God over a lifetime. She said, "We need to find God, and He cannot be found in noise and restlessness. God is the friend of silence. See how nature — trees, flowers, grass — grows in silence; see the stars, the moon and the sun, how they move in silence. . . . We need silence to be able to touch souls."[1]

It's interesting that she speaks of finding God in silence. After her death, her correspondence to her spiritual directors became public, though she had asked that it be destroyed. The letters revealed that from 1946 until just before her death, Mother Teresa suffered a dark night of the soul. In one of her letters she described "just that terrible pain of loss, of God not wanting me, of God not being God, of God not really existing."[2]

That is half a century of God's seeming silence. And yet Mother Teresa continued to love and care for the least ones in India. She didn't let feelings alter her path. She clung to the written word of God. She wasn't the mystic, spiritual giant many perceived her to be, but a struggling pilgrim working to be faithful to her Lord.

It's something we don't often talk about, fidelity — a faithfulness to God despite how we feel. Mother Teresa underwent what she considered to be a purification process during this dark night of the soul.

You've often heard that feelings — emotions — are notoriously untrustworthy. And yet so much of our faith is described in emotional terms. "I feel so close to God." Feelings are part of it, but faith is so much more than feelings. If part of your story involves your own dark nights — perhaps depression, addiction, or deep emotional wounds — you understand that sometimes our faith blossoms while God seems silent. We've come to realize that even if we don't sense Him, He's been there all the time.

FIFTEEN:
AND HE WAS NEVER
THE SAME AGAIN . . .

> Do not conform to the pattern of this
> world, but be transformed by the
> renewing of your mind. Then you will be
> able to test and approve what God's will
> is — his good, pleasing and perfect will.
> — ROMANS 12:2

Transformation. It's our favorite part of the story. When we see a character slowly changing, we know there is hope for the ending we're pulling for. We are drawn to character growth and change. For example, there's the crotchety old man whose heart softens once a child comes into his life. Remember the story *Heidi,* by Johanna Spyri? Or what about the young woman who sees nothing but arrogance and disdain in the eyes of an aristocratic suitor, only to discover that her own pride and prejudice are far greater? (Think Jane Austen.)

I was seated with a group of friends

around a table when Carole Lewis, director of First Place 4 Health, a weight loss and total health program, told a story that had us all in stitches. She began, in her Texas drawl, by asking whether she had ever told us how her cat got saved. Of course we were all ears. Yellow Cat (yes, that's his name) was the meanest cat Carole had ever seen. He would jump up on her bed, purring and stretching just like a kitty that wanted to be petted. As soon as he had suckered Carole into petting him, he'd turn and bite her hand or reach out and scratch her. Then he'd jump off the bed and hide before she could call him on his behavior. Yellow Cat was a nightmare.

Carole lives on the water in Houston, and when her family evacuated for Hurricane Ike, she brought out her two cat carriers, one for the docile Archie, the other for Yellow Cat. Well, Yellow Cat, ever stubborn and disagreeable, saw the cat carriers and refused to come. He hid somewhere, and no matter how hard they searched they couldn't find him. The winds were blowing harder and harder, and finally they knew they had to leave Yellow Cat.

After Ike, Carole was convinced Yellow Cat couldn't possibly have survived, but when they went back to the bay on Monday,

there he was in the rafters of the garage —
one of the few structures that survived. He
was still scared and refused to come down.
However, the next day, when they returned
once more, Carole placed a can of albacore
tuna inside his cat carrier. Yellow Cat was
so hungry he left his shelter. When he went
into his carrier to eat the tuna, Carole was
able to shut the door.

She told us that when she opened the carrier door in their temporary living quarters,
he was a different cat. "He got saved." She
was convinced Yellow Cat must have had a
spiritual experience during the battering of
the storm, because he emerged as the sweetest, most docile cat they'd ever seen. He's
never attempted to bite or scratch Carole
again.

We laughed until our sides hurt when
Carole told the story of her "saved" cat. But
when we talk about change, we need to
remember that even though most changes
are gradual and take a great deal of work,
sometimes a catastrophic event can bring
about change seemingly overnight.

As I write my books, I never lose sight of
the importance of character growth and
change. Often the book starts out with
characters far apart, sometimes because of
misunderstanding, sometimes because of

things that happened in the past, sometimes because of prejudice — preformed beliefs — and sometimes because of plain old stubbornness. My job as author is to take those characters through scene after scene, crisis after crisis that will slowly break down their walls and allow for the change that will facilitate a happy ending.

We're all hoping for those happy endings. What we don't realize is that transformation is the prerequisite for any story.

So, how does change happen?

ELEMENTS OF CHANGE

Instead of just talking about how change takes place with the characters I create, I want to flip over to your life story. I want to talk about how change happens for all of us. I know a lot about change because I've struggled with it in many areas of my own life — weight, time management, my relationships with people, my relationship with God, and many other areas as well. I've discovered that there are specific steps to change.

Dissatisfaction

The first step is the hardest. It's realizing you are sick of the status quo. If the status quo is being overweight, you look in the mirror with total disgust. Or you try to pull on your skinny jeans and realize the word *skinny* could never be applied to that part of your anatomy. If your status quo is a spiritual dissatisfaction, you may feel totally lost. Hopeless. You sense there must be more to life than this day-to-day grind. If your problem is an addiction of one kind or another, you reach bottom and realize there's no place left to go.

If you were to use a twelve-step program like Alcoholics Anonymous, Narcotics Anonymous, or Overeaters Anonymous, you'd discover that you must come to a point where you admit you are helpless to bring about these changes on your own. To effect lasting change, you need to call on God's help. That is excellent advice. It's probably the reason those programs are effective in so many lives.

Vision for Change

Dissatisfaction leads to a decision to make the next step — envisioning what the change will look like. When I first started to write, I decided to set a goal of finishing twenty manuscript pages each day. Then I calculated how long it would take for me to finish a book. This was good practice for what was to follow later, when I was offered a writing contract. Because I was already a disciplined writer, I knew I would be able to meet my deadlines.

Many of my friends who've battled weight issues keep a dress they wore when they were at their optimal weight. They picture themselves wearing that dress again. And many of them eventually do fit back into that dress. Visualizing our goals is an important part of the process of change.

A Workable Plan

We need to develop a workable plan for change. Emphasis on *workable.* Step by step. Little by little. If I had set a goal of writing thirty manuscript pages a day when I first started writing, it simply would have been impossible. As it was, twenty pages a day challenged me. To set a goal of thirty pages a day would be setting myself up for failure. I would have grown discouraged and frustrated with myself, and I might have thrown in the towel and lost out on a wonderful career.

It's the same with weight loss. If losing weight was the change you were seeking and you set a goal of five pounds a week, you'd be setting yourself up for failure. One of my favorite weight-loss specialists is Carole Lewis, director of First Place 4 Health. She says, "We do not want our members to lose more than two pounds a week because it is physiologically impossible to lose more than two pounds of *fat* in that short a time."

Don't forget that change needs to take place at a pace that will allow for the new behavior to become a permanent habit. Many self-help gurus say that it takes twenty-eight days for something to become a habit. I'm skeptical about setting an exact number of days, since we are all different, but I agree that when we practice the behavior of change over and over it becomes our new normal.

Working the Plan

It's great to have a plan for transformation, but the rubber meets the road when it comes to working the plan. The term *working the plan* represents the tough part — it means implementing your intention. Let's say you long to live in a clean, clutter-free home. The only problem is that you are a card-carrying messy person. You've developed a workable plan — you are going to tackle one room every Saturday until the house is organized and free of clutter. Excellent plan. The only problem is that Saturday comes along, the sun is shining, and it's a perfect day to go yard sale road-tripping with friends. Do you work your plan or abandon it to go find more clutter? This is where the vision comes in. Which do you want more, the clean, organized house or a day of play? It comes down to how strong your dissatisfaction was in the first place.

If you work the plan, the end result will be that wonderful feeling of accomplishment that comes from an organized, clean space. If you set aside the plan, you'll end up feeling guilty and defeated.

The truth is, implementing change takes discipline. I keep going back to that important step of admitting we are helpless on our own. We need to constantly pray for strength and resolve, for the determination to keep our needs in mind. One small decision will often lead to another. As a benefit, our decision-making muscles grow stronger with every positive action we take.

Celebrating the Change

But when change happens, we need to take time to celebrate. We live in such a busy world that we often just move from one challenge to the next without stopping to appreciate where we have been and to recognize where we are now. I'm a believer in celebrating, and I make time to do so, whether that means celebrating milestones like birthdays or Christmas or celebrating people. Acknowledging achievements is one of the best kinds of celebrations we can have. We aren't necessarily patting ourselves on the back; we're telling God how grateful we are for His help, for seeing us through. You can bet He's celebrating with us. He's a proud Father eager to tell each one of us, "Well done!"

In the Old Testament, the people celebrated victories or times when God intervened by stopping to build an altar. For a nomadic people, erecting a tribute of stones was a significant act. I talk a little about altar building and how it applies to us on page 238.

But when you've achieved change, or even have taken an important step toward your eventual goal, celebrate. Include your family and friends. You just might inspire them as well.

AGENTS OF CHANGE

Let's go back to talking about transformation in literary characters. Not all characters in stories change. Sometimes a character is simply an agent *of* change. Someone pointed out that Anne of Green Gables is such a character. She doesn't really change. She stays the same — wise beyond her years, prone to mishaps, an overachiever, and fiercely loyal — throughout a series of eight books by Lucy Maud Montgomery. It is those around her who change. The same could be said about the children's classic *Pollyanna,* by Eleanor Porter. The title character plays the "glad game," and while she remains the same, others see life in a new light through the eyes of this little girl who views life as a positive.

The wise old men and women in stories are also often agents of change. They dispense wisdom and enter into the characters' lives as mentors but rarely change themselves. I think of Atticus Finch in *To Kill a Mockingbird.*

In real life, Jesus Christ was an agent of change. He came into the world without sin and left the world the same way. No change needed. But everyone He touched changed in one way or another. His disciples became far more than they ever dreamed of becoming. We're talking about men like Simon Peter, who was nothing more than a fisherman trying to eke a living out of the sea. No education, no résumé, but he became a world changer, and our Church was built on him.

Not many of us can be that agent of change as easily as any one of Jesus's disciples, but I'm guessing you are an agent of change in some area of your life. If you are a parent, you are an agent of change to your children. If you are a teacher, you are changing lives every day — we need only think back on the teachers of our youth and the influence they had on our lives to understand how. If you are in ministry, you will be changing lives in the most profound way — for eternity.

CHANGE TAKES TIME

We already talked about the time it takes for a change to become permanent, but we need to recognize that some changes take time — a long time. I suffered a huge setback in my life when Dale died. I'm still grieving his loss. For me to say that I'll give myself a year or two years to accept the change to our family structure would be ridiculous. I will forever mourn his loss and see his empty place at family functions and holiday dinners as I watch his sons grow into manhood.

Any transformation takes time. I think of my friends who've been widowed. To lose a best friend and a life partner is a change that forever shapes their futures. Rather than chart a change that calls for you to "get on with your life," it would make more sense to set realistic goals, like "Find one fun thing to do every Saturday," or "Make a dinner date with friends every week."

I'm new to deep grief, and it's still raw, but I'm guessing we never get over the loss, we just find new joys and develop our own workarounds to make life meaningful. I've buried both my parents, but their deaths were anticipated. One doesn't ever expect to bury a child. This is new territory for Wayne and me, and a difficult road often filled with ruts and detours.

When Wayne broke his arm, the doctor told us it would take six to eight weeks to heal. Grief is completely different. There is no set time when one can say, "Okay, it's been long enough. I'm over that now. Time to move on."

CHARTING CHANGE

We come around to my journals again. It is important to record our lives, and transformation is a part of that life experience. Make sure to record your journey to change. If your goal is weight loss, you'll want to keep charts of the loss so you can easily look back on them and see where you started and how far you've come. It's too easy to get impatient, so it is even more important to be able to look back and celebrate how far we've come.

The thing to remember is this: change is often painful, and it can be excruciatingly slow, but without transformation, without change, there's no way to get to the happy ending.

Storytelling Prompt
Looking back on your life, name some turning points. Finish the sentence, "If it hadn't been for _____, I never would have _____." What was your most profound life change? What brought it on? How did it change you?

Ready for a Change

We were created for change. There are 2.5 trillion red blood cells in a human body at any one moment. Because cells need to be replaced, 2.5 million new red blood cells need to be produced every second by the bone morrow. That's like creating the population of Chicago every second. That's a lot of change. Nothing stays the same. Our bodies begin to shrink at the age of thirty. And did you know that every month we grow a brand-new layer of skin? It reminds me of the David Bowie song, "Changes."

We are constantly changing in other ways as well — spiritually, intellectually, emotionally, and physically. The question is, do we change only in response to events that happen to us, or do we seek change on our own terms?

You can use story techniques to chart your own transformation. Here are some steps:

1. Think about what your "ordinary world" looks like.
2. Decide how you would like it to be different.
3. Write the story as you imagine it could be. Don't buy into someone else's story. It's too easy to say, "I want to be rich, working in the perfect job, seeing each of my children grow up successful . . ." Dig deeper.
4. Make sure you are writing the change you want to see in yourself. If you begin talking about changes for other people in your story, you're going to be stymied.
5. If you seek to transform into the kind of person God wants you to be, you need to listen for His voice. How do you hear that? By spending

time silently with Him, Bible in hand; by studying what He had to say in His love letter to us — the Bible; by seeking the advice of your wise mentors.

6. Chart the steps needed to become the character in the story you've written.

7. Take the first step toward change.

8. Journal the process. You'll discover much more about yourself if you chronicle the process. Remember, the process is usually much more important than the outcome.

Sixteen:
Happily Ever After . . .

But those who hope in the Lord
will renew their strength.
They will soar on wings like eagles;
they will run and not grow weary,
they will walk and not be faint.

— ISAIAH 40:31

Don't we love those happy endings in books?

Many writers, especially those who write literary fiction — that fiction where the writing style is almost more important than the story — prefer to write tragic endings. They'll argue that it's more realistic and that most people don't get to experience many happy endings. But guess what? Those of us who write books with happy endings outsell the others by huge margins. My feeling is that the reader is making an emotional investment when they read one of my books. I owe them a story that will lift their spirits, remind them that there is goodness to life, and leave them with a sense of hope and joy.

My readers aren't alone. We all long for happy endings. The nice thing is that God plans a happy ending for us. We will all die eventually. That sounds final, doesn't it? Well, it's not. It's just the beginning.

Frederick Buechner tells us the "final secret" in his book *Listening to Your Life.* Here's what he says: "And the promise is that, yes, on the weary feet of faith and the fragile wings of hope, we will come to love at last as from the first He has loved us — loved us even in the wilderness, especially in the wilderness, because He has been in the wilderness with us."[1]

We have a lot of wilderness to get through before we reach that Promised Land. These images come from the Old Testament story of Moses and the children of Israel. You remember the story, right? The Israelites were held captive, were slaves in Egypt for four hundred years. They spent their days under the thumb of the Egyptians, futilely trying to make bricks without the straw that was needed to bind the clay mixture. And they were building for the Egyptians, ever building. They longed for freedom.

PLAGUES AND PESTILENCE

God called a reluctant Moses to free his people. (God's own reluctant hero!) Obtaining their freedom was not an easy task. It took plagues and pestilence and finally death to convince the pharaoh to let Moses lead his people to the Promised Land. Pharaoh grudgingly let them go, but after a short time revisited this decision. After all, he had just dispatched his entire workforce. By all reckoning, the total number of Israelites in the Exodus was probably close to two million. Others joined the Exodus as well, maybe even some Egyptians and other slaves. Pharaoh must have looked at the stacks of drying bricks and the partially completed granaries in the storehouse cities of Pithom and Ramses and changed his mind.

MIRACLE AFTER MIRACLE

Led by a cloud by day and a pillar of fire by night, these ex-slaves took a roundabout route to keep themselves safe from the threat of war with the much-feared Philistines.

Pharaoh led an entire regiment to bring them back, six hundred of his best chariots, along with other chariots, with officers over all of them. A staggering, impressive force.

As the thundering of the Egyptian forces announced their approach, the people camped along the banks of the Red Sea became afraid and berated Moses for bringing them out of Egypt.

But God wasn't done with miracles. Moses stretched out his hand over the sea as instructed by God, and the waters opened like a valley in the sea — it must have been a half-mile wide to accommodate two million people. And here's something else I find impressive: they walked across on *dry land.* Can you imagine what it must have been like for them, looking at the walls of water on either side of their path?

As the Egyptians followed, God threw their entire army into disarray. First the wheels began jamming or coming off their chariots, causing them to career into one another. Then, as they entered the dry path in the Red Sea where the children of Israel had just passed, Moses once again obediently held up his arm, and the waters closed over the path, drowning the army of the pharaoh.

GRUMBLING AND GROANING

With all those miracles behind them you'd think the people would forever follow Moses and his God, Jehovah. But they were human, and as time passed and they wandered in the wilderness, they began grumbling and growing impatient. Believe it or not, they began to yearn for Egypt, the very place of their enslavement. They remembered the rich foods they'd often had and compared those to the manna and quail God provided for them now. They yearned for the variety of Egyptian fare, even if it came with cruel enslavement. (Food issues are obviously not a new phenomenon.)

And when they reached the very border of the Promised Land, scouts were sent to give a report. They reported back that the land was good indeed — flowing with milk and honey. But they also reported that the land was populated with giants, men who made them look like grasshoppers. Joshua and Caleb countered this report, reminding the people that if God promised the land, they had nothing to fear.

Unfortunately, the people bought into the worst-case scenario. In fact, they went as far as attempting to stone Caleb and Joshua. The people's lack of faith angered the Lord so deeply that if Moses hadn't intervened on their behalf, begging God for mercy, the Lord would have just plain struck them down. Instead, God forgave them, but the consequence of their lack of faith was that none of them would ever see the land promised to their forefathers. That would be left to their children.

And so they wandered.

LIFE IN OUR WILDERNESS

The reason I retell that story is that it's not so very different from our life experience. Despite the miracles we see around us, much of our life is spent wandering in the wilderness. I've experienced many a miracle in my day. The birth of each child. The unexplained success of my career. The parking spot that miraculously opens up right near the entrance to the mall on Black Friday. But I have to admit that like the wandering Jews, I sometimes let the daily grind get to me and grumble just as much as they did. I forget to look up.

NAVIGATING THE WILDERNESS

As we make our way to our own happy endings, we have a lot of wilderness to cross. Some of the things that will help us navigate that wilderness can be found in the story of the Exodus. Here are some principles:

- **Look to the future.** We need to leave Egypt and not look back. Your Egypt is whatever enslaved you before you were set free. Each one of us needs to identify those things that enslaved us and turn them over to the Lord. Freedom is what He promises us.

- **Accept the journey.** Sometimes we are called to wander. For some of us, the Promised Land will not come in this life. I think of so many who are persecuted around the world, and some of us who carry almost unbearable burdens each day. Believe it or not, our job is to worship God in the wilderness. He promises that "those who hope in the Lord will renew their strength. They will soar on wings like eagles; they will run and not grow weary, they will walk and not be faint" (Isa. 40:31).

- **Fear not.** The Israelites tried to turn back when things got scary. We need to look hard at our lives. Is there something we've been called to do, but when it looked too hard or too scary, we turned back? I've watched so many aspiring writers give up when someone told them how hard it would be to get an agent and then how difficult it would be to land a publishing contract. Fortunately, God doesn't call us to something for which He will not equip us. That's just what He said to Moses when the people were too afraid to enter the Promised Land.

HAPPY TRAILS TO YOU

We may have many happy endings in our lives. Ours may be a love story with a happy ending. Our children may end up being jewels in our crown — the perfect happy ending. (Okay, there may be a lot of wilderness before the happy ending with kids.) Our jobs may have a happy ending.

But other things in our lives may be cliffhangers. I know some who had miserable childhoods, full of abuse; they never got that moment of closure with the abuser. Or some of us have lost a loved one way too early. We never got to see their happy endings. Our own lives may be cut short. I think of all the letters I've received from cancer patients who've read my books while going through chemotherapy treatment. I work with World Vision, an organization dedicated to caring for children the world over, and I've become aware of the children in Africa who are orphaned by the AIDS epidemic. They call those orphaned children "child-headed households." It means little children huddled together with no parent and no adult caregiver.

THE ETERNAL VIEW

The good news is that this earthly life is not all there is. As French Jesuit priest Pierre Teilhard de Chardin said, "We are not human beings having a spiritual experience; we are spiritual beings having a human experience." Our time on earth is just a small part of our lives. The happy ending comes when we cross over.

One of the best books I've read on life after death is Randy Alcorn's *Heaven*. He simply takes all the verses in the Bible that refer to heaven and builds a clear picture of what it's going to be like. Once you've learned what the Bible has to say about the New Earth, you'll never view it the same way again.

C. S. Lewis, in *The Last Battle,* one of the books in his Narnia series, sums it up best as the children, Peter, Lucy, and Edmund cross over into the afterlife. He says, "But for them it was only the beginning of the real story. All their life in this world and all their adventures in Narnia had only been the cover and the title page: now at last they were beginning Chapter One of the Great Story which no one on earth has read: which goes on forever; in which every chapter is better than the one before."[2]

So as you write your own story, keep in mind that this is only the cover and the title page of your story. Our stories will stretch out to eternity.

THE PREREQUISITE TO THE HAPPY ENDING

We are all eternal beings. Ecclesiastes 3:11 says we have eternity in our hearts. And we will all stand before the throne of God someday. All of our actions will be played out. I picture it as a movie screen, and I'm guessing that it will be terribly uncomfortable to have all that played out for everyone to see. But when it comes to the judgment, if we've made the decision in this life to follow Christ, He'll step forward as our advocate and say that His sacrifice paid the debt for all those sins. It'll be like they never happened.

But if the person standing before the throne rejected Christ, or didn't intentionally seek Him during his life on earth, there will be no one to stand for him, and sadly, sadly, he'll not be able to enter.

Just as I provide happy endings for all the stories I write, I long for happy endings to all those lost ones' life stories as well. I long for a happy ending to your life story, too.

What will your life look like after you leave this earth? Can you describe your eternal home? Can you picture what it will be like? What you will be doing?

Altar Building

In the Old Testament, God often commanded his people to build an altar. The altar was a place of worship, a place to offer a sacrifice to God, a place to commemorate God's work among the people. In most accounts of altar building, the wording is, "He built an altar to the Lord." The altar was an act of offering as well as a place where offerings were received. The biblical accounts of altar building are fascinating. Noah built them, and Abraham, Isaac, Jacob, Moses, David, Daniel, and Elijah did as well.

As the story of the Bible — our story, really — unwinds, we see that Adam and Eve were created to be companions to God. He delighted in them and spent time with them every day. They were sinless until they decided they wanted more and reached out for forbidden fruit. The only thing God cannot look upon is sin, so they had to give up the intimate relationship they had with Him. They had to leave the beautiful garden and set out on their perilous journey back to God — a different kind of hero's journey.

God was not willing to turn His back on them forever. He devised a way for them to be cleansed, and it came through the complicated sacrifice of an animal's blood — often a lamb's blood. This act of sacrifice took place on those very stone altars. Adam and Eve's descendants didn't fully understand that the shedding of lamb's blood was a foreshadowing of the greatest sacrifice of all time — the shedding of Jesus's blood.

Once Jesus came and died as our sacrifice, we no longer had to build stone altars and sacrifice animals. (Can you imagine getting that by animal rights activists these days?) We live on the other side of the sacrifice. All we do is accept the once-for-all-time sacrifice of Jesus.

In *My Utmost for His Highest,* Oswald Chambers puts it this way: "The heart of salvation is the Cross of Christ. The reason salvation is so easy to obtain is that it cost God so much. The Cross was the place where God and sinful man merged with a tremendous collision and where the way to life was opened. But all the cost and pain of the collision was absorbed by the heart of God."[3]

We build different altars these days. The altars we build to the Lord are worship, prayer, and praise. An altar is always a place where we intentionally seek God. My altar may look like a kitchen table, but every morning I go there to pray, study, and seek that intimate relationship with my Lord. Sometimes it is a place of refuge — a place where I go simply to be silent before Him.

Building an altar — a place where one can intentionally seek God — is an act that enhances the life of the builder. You may carve your altar out of the corner of a room, set up a place in the garden, or make a space by your bedside, but whatever place you set aside, it will become one of your favorite spots to pull away from life and offer the sacrifice of time with the One who delights in you.

"The LORD delights in those who fear him, who put their hope in his unfailing love" (Ps. 147:11).

SEVENTEEN:
AND IF HE'S NOT GONE,
HE LIVES THERE STILL . . .

But whoever drinks the water
I give them will never thirst.
Indeed, the water I give them will become
in them a spring of water welling
up to eternal life.
— JOHN 4:14

In the last chapter we talked about the happy endings of our stories, but guess what? Our story is actually open-ended. We don't type, "The End."

Long after we leave this earth, our stories live on in the hearts, and sometimes in the hands, of others. There are so many ways to tell your story.

MEMORIES

Many of our stories will be told, after we are gone, in the memories of those we touched. Think of your own memories. Do you remember spending time with your grandmother? I'm very intentional in spending time with my grandchildren. I want to be sure they have many happy memories of me.

A few years back I took my three granddaughters to New York City, where we shared one bathroom for the four of us. My turn finally came — ten minutes of pure, uninterrupted peace, at last! I climbed into the shower. I wasn't in there one minute before Jazmine knocked at the door. "Grandma, I need to get something." Another knock, Maddie: "Sorry, Grandma, I have to go." Knock, knock . . . Bailey came in: "Everyone's in here; I was lonely."

It's those kinds of memories we look back on with laughter. After I'm gone, I pray my children and grandchildren will remember me as available to them no matter what. I believe building memories with my grandchildren is so important to me because I don't have any memories of my grandmothers. Both died before I had the opportunity to know them. And yet they are very much a part of me. My love of craft came from my paternal grandmother. My older cousins tell stories of watching her crochet in her rocking chair, rocking away, asleep and snoring but never missing a stitch. I, unfortunately, missed seeing that, but I was the one who inherited a love of yarn. My maternal grandmother was a wonderful cook who was able to create amazing meals with limited resources in the heart of the Great Depression. A little bacon grease, a few potatoes and other vegetables, and she managed to put together a feast.

ACTS OF KINDNESS

Hopefully we'll be remembered for our acts of kindness. My friend told me about the funeral of a timid bachelor farmer in her church. When the pastor asked if anyone had something they'd like to share about him, she worried that no one would have anything to say. He was so quiet. So unassuming. But one person after another came to the front to tell stories of his generosity. They spoke of how he helped others survive financially when they were at their lowest point. They told of how he'd helped them get their harvest in when rain threatened. He loaned equipment when needed, or paid a doctor's bill. He signed for a loan, invested in a business, purchased groceries, and mowed the lawn of an invalid. The memories went on. No one had known about any of these acts, and everyone realized that it wasn't until that day that a picture of the real man emerged.

In this digital age I wonder if we're losing too much of our correspondence. Letters have always been a wonderful way to leave a bit of ourselves behind. Some of the autographs I collect come at the bottom of a letter or a piece of correspondence. Letters are such personal things.

Like the letter J. R. R. Tolkien sent to his son, Christopher Tolkien, on October 25, 1944. He wrote:

Dearest man,
Here is a little more of "the Ring" for your delectation (I hope) and criticism. . . . Two more chapters to complete the "Fourth Book" and then I hope to finish the "Fifth" and last of the Ring. I have written a long airletter today, and shall write again (of course) before your birthday. I'm afraid this little packet won't get to you in time for it. . . . God bless you, beloved. Do you think "The Ring" will come off, and reach the thirsty?

Your own Father[1]

A letter like that, filled with love, showing the heart of the letter writer, is priceless. Especially when the letter is by an author we revere and about a story we love.

I receive hundreds of reader letters. These are important to me, and I make them a priority. Each letter that comes into my office is answered. So many of the letters and comments on my online guestbook are personal and heartfelt. I keep these, and sometimes share them with Wayne and others in the publishing house or in my office. I do this because without Wayne's encouragement and support I would never have been able to achieve my dream of being a published author. The ones I share with my editor are special as well. My editor has often put many hours into a project. When readers praise me, they are also praising her work on the book, and she deserves to know that her efforts are appreciated.

JOURNALS

As you surely know by now, I'm a huge proponent of journaling. I've kept a journal or a diary ever since the time I could first write. I often tell the story about how my brother and two of my cousins made copies of my diary and sold it to the boys in my eighth-grade class. (It was my first bestseller, unfortunately.)

Over the years I've used my journals to record my life and to work out my struggles, to talk to God. I pour out my joys and anxieties on the empty white pages. I've been unflinchingly honest, so I'm not sure whether these journals will be handed down to my children or burned upon my passing. But for me they've been a way to work out my life, to know what I'm thinking and to see how God is working through me. I can look back on them and see His fingerprints on every page. A journal gives us a long view of life. A bird's-eye view.

Many journals have become treasured parts of our literature. I think of the diary of Anne Frank. Anne was so transparent, so vulnerable on the pages of her diary. I'm sure she never intended anyone but her imaginary Kitty to read it, but with her diary she personalized the Holocaust. On Tuesday, March 7, 1944, she wrote, "Beauty remains, even in misfortune. If you just look for it, you discover more and more happiness. . . . A person who has courage and faith will never die in misery!" [2]

PHOTOGRAPHS

Our photographs capture memories and portray places far better than words can. How many times have you pored over a box of fading photographs, wondering about the lives of those pictured? One of the things almost all of us intend to do is be more intentional about photographs — writing the names of people and places and dates on the backs. Otherwise, as time goes on, memories fade, and soon it will be difficult to place the details.

The practice of scrapbooking has remedied that for many. The scrapbooks I've seen combine words and photos artfully, telling a complete story. These will be treasured for generations.

And now, creating digital books has become easy and relatively inexpensive. Almost anyone can go to a Web site, upload photos, and create a beautiful printed book of personal photographs for a relatively modest price. It's a great way to tell your story in a photojournalistic way.

RECIPES

Food is an important part of my life. I love to cook, and I love to feed people. Okay, I'll admit it, I'm a foodie. I've long collected recipes, created recipes, and shared recipes with readers and friends. One of my favorite things is to find an interesting new recipe and head to the kitchen to try it out. I have recipes from my mother, my aunts, my grandmother, dear friends, and my children. My recipe box holds memories of food, people, and great occasions. It's definitely part of my story.

I have a friend whose octogenarian mother spent a whole year typing out the family recipes, copying them, and putting them into beautiful binders, one for each member of the family. The recipe pages are filled with pithy sayings and notes about when the family used to enjoy a particular recipe. Now that she is gone, her family treasures those books.

CREATIVE WORKS

The work of your hands becomes an important legacy as well. When I'm knitting, I spend most of that time thinking about and praying for the person who will receive the sweater, vest, scarf, or hat. Just a week before I wrote this, Cindy DeBerry, a dear friend of mine from school days, died. I couldn't attend the funeral because I was away at a conference. But other friends who went told me that Cindy was buried with the sweater I knit for her. To me, knitting and loving are intertwined. Creating lovely handcrafted pieces is one way I express love.

It's the same with so many pieces of needlework. Quilts fascinate me. So many of them tell a story. If you are a quilter, you are telling your story with every piece and each stitch. Whatever you create, it's part of your legacy. We need to make sure our children and grandchildren understand some of what goes into our creations so they can appreciate the legacy even more.

THE GREATEST STORY OF ALL

Throughout the pages of this book we've talked about Story. We've taken it apart and looked at the individual parts that make it up. I've shared how I write my books and how I tell stories, and we've looked at your own story. I've encouraged you to tell your story — to look at your life as one grand adventure and to see God's hand on your life and in your story.

But the most amazing story of all belongs to all of us. It's a love story. The story of God — the one true God — and His love affair with a wayward and obstinate people. (That's us.) It doesn't begin with "once upon a time," but if we think in terms of the classic hero's journey, the ordinary world in this story journey was a garden so lush and exquisite we cannot even imagine it. Then something happened — a snake, a piece of forbidden fruit, and a terrible decision — and God's beloved people were cast onto their journey, naked and ashamed.

The Bible tells the story of trouble,

trouble, and more trouble along the way. It also tells the story of rescue, and people reaching out toward the God they could barely remember. The God who loved them so much.

Things couldn't have gotten much worse, but then God sent the ultimate sacrifice into the world, His very own much-loved Son, Jesus, who came as a baby and grew to be a man, walking, talking, and dealing with people just as we have done. The final challenge in the story happened on a lonely, windswept hill called Golgotha, where God's Son was put to death — not for anything He did but as the final payment for the sin that started with that forbidden piece of fruit. His tomb represents the ultimate deepest, darkest cave, but thankfully the story didn't end there. That cave could not hold Him.

That sacrifice was the key that unlocked the door that stood between God and those obstinate people. All we have to do to find our eternal happily ever after is walk through that door. It sounds too simplistic, but trust me, that's all we have to do. The Lord said, "Here I am! I stand at the door and knock. If anyone hears my voice and opens the door, I will come in and eat with that person, and they with me" (Rev. 3:20). True intimacy restored.

If following Jesus is something you'd like to do, if rediscovering intimacy with God sounds like what you've been yearning for, all you need to do is walk through that door and set out on your own story journey.

I promise you, it'll be a grand adventure.

Our story goes on long after we have crossed over. We need to be intentional about leaving a trail for those who follow. I want the generations who follow to know that, more than my books and more than my knitting and cooking, I determined to faithfully serve the Lord. I want them to choose to follow Him, and so I'm intentional about leaving a legacy of faith as well as a legacy of memories.

Storytelling Prompt

You have most of the story still ahead of you, both temporal and eternal. Tell what you've learned that will stand you in good stead for the rest of the story. What kinds of stories will you leave behind?

Telling Your Story

Throughout the pages of this book I've encouraged you to discover your story and find ways to share it. You might use some of the storytelling prompts at the end of each chapter to share your story in a group setting. You might begin to record your story in your journal. Perhaps you've decided to work on your verbal storytelling skills with friends and family. Even if none of these appeals to you, I pray that I've helped you see your life from a different perspective — as one divine, never-ending story.

I've shared some of my own story in the pages of this book. I would consider it a blessing to hear your stories as well. Please feel free to write to me at P.O. Box 1458, Port Orchard, WA, 98366. Many of my readers use the guestbook at my Web site to write to me. You can find that at www.DebbieMacomber.com.

As I think of you, my readers, and your stories, let me close with the words of Paul from 1 Thessalonians. They reflect how I feel about you.

"It is clear to us, friends, that God not only loves you very much but has also put his hand on you for something special" (1:4; The Message).

Something special indeed. I look forward to hearing what you discover.

NOTES

One. In the Beginning . . .

1. Madeleine L'Engle, *The Rock That Is Higher: Story as Truth* (Wheaton, IL: Harold Shaw, 1993), 215.
2. E. M. Forster, *Aspects of the Novel* (New York: Harcourt Brace & Company, 1927), 26–27.
3. Madeleine L'Engle, *Walking on Water* (Wheaton, IL: Harold Shaw, 1980, 1998, 2001), 24.
4. Madeleine L'Engle, *Madeleine L'Engle Herself: Reflections on a Writing Life* (Colorado Springs: Waterbrook, 2001), 85.
5. Mark Batterson, *Soulprint: Discovering Your Divine Destiny* (Colorado Springs: Multnomah, 2011), 46.
6. Ibid., 62.

Two. In a Land Far Away . . .

1. C. S. Lewis, *Surprised by Joy: The Shape of My Early Life* (New York: Harcourt Brace Jovanovich, 1956), 7.
2. Ibid., 16.
3. http://www.brainyquote.com/quotes/quotes/g/grahamgree166575.html.
4. Meg Leder, Jack Heffron, and the Editors of *Writer's Digest, The Complete Handbook of Novel Writing* (Cincinnati: Writer's Digest Books, 2002), 431.
5. Ibid., 435.

Three. In the Days . . .

1. Anne Lamott, *Bird by Bird: Some Instructions on Writing and Life* (New York: Pantheon Books, 1994), 34.
2. Ibid., 4.

Four. There Once Was a Man . . .

1. Penelope J. Stokes, *The Complete Guide to Writing and Selling the Christian Novel* (Cincinnati: Writer's Digest Books, 1998), 99–100.
2. George Sayer, *Jack: A Life of C. S. Lewis* (Wheaton, IL: Crossway Books, 1994), xx.
3. Frederick Buechner, *Listening to Your Life: Daily Meditations with Frederick Buechner*

(San Francisco: Harper San Francisco, 1992), 10.

Five. And He Went by the Name of . . .

1. http://www.quotationspage.com/quote/ 35879.html.
2. L.M. Montgomery, *Anne of Green Gables* (Stationer's Hall, London, L. C. Page & Company, 1908), 31,32.
3. Ibid., 78.
4. Maurice Merleau-Ponty, *Phenomenology of Perception,* trans. C. Smith (New York: The Humanities Press, 1962), 177–78.

Eight. He Tucked the Treasure Deep in His Sack . . .

1. Suzanne Labarre, "12 Hand-Written Love Letters from Famous People, from Henry VIII to Michael Jordan," *Fast Company,* last modified February 14, 2012, http://www.fastcodesign.com/1669022/12-hand-written-love-letters-from-famous-people-from-henry-viii-to-michael-jordan.
2. Debbie Macomber, *Susannah's Garden* (Don Mills, Ontario, Canada: Mira Books, 2006).

Nine. He Picked Up the Sword . . .

1. "Quotes by Barton, Bruce," Quotations Book.com, accessed December 11, 2012, http://quotationsbook.com/quotes/author/507.
2. C. S. Lewis, *God in the Dock: Essays on Theology and Ethics,* edited by Walter Hooper (Grand Rapids, MI: Eerdmans, 1970), 93.
3. Frederick Buechner, *Listening to Your Life: Daily Meditations with Frederick Buechner* (San Francisco: Harper San Francisco, 1992), 186.

Eleven. An Old Man Sat by the Side of the Road . . .

1. Kevin Bennett, "Proud Volunteer: 100-Year-Old Keeps Serving Her Community," *Aberdeen News,* November 6, 2011.
2. "Who Mentored Oprah Winfrey?" Who Mentored You, accessed December 11, 2012, http://www.hsph.harvard.edu/chc/wmy/Celebrities/oprah_winfrey.html.
3. "The Mentor Leader Quotes," Goodreads, accessed December 11, 2012, http://www.goodreads.com/work/quotes/13165457-the-mentor-leader-secrets-to

-building-people-and-teams-that-win
-consist.

Twelve. The Unseen World Gathered . . .

1. Peter Fenwick and Elizabeth Fenwick, *The Art of Dying* (London: Continuum, 2008), 30.
2. Mona Simpson, "A Sister's Eulogy for Steve Jobs," *New York Times,* October 30, 2011, http://www.nytimes.com/2011/10/30/opinion/mona-simpsons-eulogy-for-steve-jobs.html.

Thirteen. Trouble Was Bound to Come . . .

1. Chris Tiegreen, *The One Year Walk with God Devotional: Wisdom from the Bible to Renew Your Mind* (Wheaton, IL: Tyndale House Publishers, 2004).
2. Mark Batterson, *Soulprint: Discovering Your Divine Destiny* (Colorado Springs: Multnomah, 2011), 40.
3. http://seekingspirit.ca/introducing-my-friend-carol-kent.

Fourteen. And the Challenge of His Life Loomed . . .

1. "Mother Teresa Quotes," BrainyQuote, accessed December 16, 2012, http://

www.brainyquote.com/quotes/authors/m/
mother_teresa.html#jyD0tlMgFPFkvDdo.
99.

2. Carol Zaleski, "The Dark Night of
Mother Teresa," *First Things,* May 2003,
http://www.firstthings.com/article/2007/
08/the-dark-night-of-mother-teresa-42.

Sixteen. Happily Ever After . . .

1. Frederick Buechner, *Listening to Your Life*
(San Francisco: Harper San Francisco,
1992), 162.

2. C.S. Lewis, *The Last Battle* (Norwalk,
CT: The Easton Press [with permission of
HarperCollins], 1984), 210–11.

3. Oswald Chambers, *My Utmost for His
Highest* (Grand Rapids, MI: Discovery
House, 1995).

**Seventeen. And If He's Not Gone, He
Lives There Still . . .**

1. Rosalie Maggio, *How They Said It: Wise
and Witty Letters from the Famous and Infa-
mous* (Paramus, NJ: Prentice Hall, 2000),
92.

2. Anne Frank, *The Diary of a Young Girl,
The Definitive Edition* (New York: Bantam,
1997), 208.

ONCE UPON A TIME:
READING GROUP GUIDE

In *Once Upon a Time: Discovering Our Forever After Story,* bestselling author Debbie Macomber explains to readers that all of our lives are part of God's grand narrative, a never-ending story that He writes for us each and every day. Using the metaphor of storytelling — and giving some insight into her own writing process along the way — Debbie Macomber teaches readers the value of examining one's own life in order to understand God's loving presence. *Once Upon a Time* helps readers answer the questions *Who am I? Who am I called to be?* — and leaves us with some practical advice for discovering our own story as Debbie Macomber shares her incredible journey.

DISCUSSION QUESTIONS

1. Discuss the significance of the title — *Once Upon a Time.* How does the title indicate the direction this book will take?

Why does the author love the phrase "once upon a time" so much? What feeling(s) does the phrase give you?

2. On page 18 the author writes: "I was born to be a storyteller." What do you think God has called you to be? How do you know, and at what age did you discover your calling?

3. Throughout the story, the author quotes many famous authors discussing their craft. On page 24, for example, she quotes American fiction writer, journalist, and essayist Joan Didion: "Had I been blessed with even limited access to my own mind, there would have been no reason to write. I write entirely to find out what I am thinking, what I am looking at, what it means." Do you think this same quote can be applied to faith — that we need faith in order to understand ourselves, our world, and the deeper meaning of both?

4. Much of *Once Upon a Time* discusses the need to "live intentionally." What does it mean to you to live with intention? In addition to writing down our story, what else can we do to live intentionally each day?

5. At the end of Chapter 1, the author quotes Deuteronomy 4:9: "Only be careful, and watch yourselves closely so that you do not forget the things your eyes have seen or let them fade from your heart as long as you live. Teach them to your children and to their children after them." In light of this quote, discuss with your group the importance of memory. Why do we cherish our memories? What memories do you hold most dear, and why?

6. For the author, the moment that she realized her future was during a visit to a library. When did that "one moment in childhood when the door opens and lets the future in" (44) occur for you? Describe where you were, who you were with, and what you were doing in that moment.

7. Reread the description of the importance of names in the Bible, beginning on page 77. Afterwards, share the meaning of your own name with your group. How does the meaning of your name reflect the person you are or the person you are called to be?

8. On page 105, the author poses an important question: "If there wasn't a single

obstacle blocking your path, what would you be doing?" Spend some quiet reflection time individually pondering this question. Then share with your group your answer(s). What is it that you want for your life above all else?

9. Chapter 8 is all about treasures — physical and otherwise. Just as characters in novels have treasures or artifacts meant to symbolize something important about who they are and where they have come from, so do we fill our homes with items that speak to some aspect of our core selves. Have a show-and-tell with your group, selecting an item in your house that best symbolizes something about you. Share the item and tell why it is so important to your story.

10. "As iron sharpens iron, so one person sharpens another" (Proverbs 27:17). Discuss a relationship in your life that has shaped who you are today. What relationship do you think the author felt most shaped her?

11. Conflict is part of any good story — and certainly part of our lives. "Where there is potential conflict, there is potential

for great growth" (192), writes Debbie Macomber. Do you agree? Think back to a time of conflict in your life. How did you grow as a result of this conflict?

12. Revisit the moment when the author shares the story of her son Dale's death, beginning on page 204. How does she find the strength to continue with her life and her writing after such an event?

13. What would you name as the major theme of this book? Why do you think that the author, Debbie Macomber, feels so strongly that her readers should share their story?

ADDITIONAL ACTIVITIES: WAYS OF ENHANCING YOUR BOOK CLUB

1. At the end of each chapter, *Once Upon a Time* offers storytelling prompts for sharing your story. Over dinner, participate in the ancient tradition of oral storytelling. Choose one or two prompts and share with your group. Afterwards, discuss with your group any surprises or insights you learned about the members of your book club. What did these stories teach you about your friends — and yourself?

2. Follow Debbie Macomber's advice and write your own story. Start a journal or a scrapbook — whichever you prefer — and try to write or create one entry per day for an entire year. It can be one line or one photo, or a longer entry, but be sure to capture the details of your everyday life. What lessons did you learn about yourself? Did anything surprise you?

3. In Chapter 14 the author discusses dark nights — times in life when God seems nowhere to be found. The poem "Dark Night of the Soul" by John of the Cross captures the spirit of this feeling. Read the poem out loud to your group: http://www .poetry-chaikhana.com/J/JohnoftheCro/ DarkNight.htm. Pick out your favorite line and write it on a piece of a paper. Using that line, compose a poem of your own that describes a dark time in your life when it was difficult to feel God's love. Share your poems with your group, explaining the context of your own "dark night."

4. Can't get enough of Debbie Macomber? Try reading some of her fiction with your book club, such as the Cedar Cove series. What are similar themes you find in both

her fiction and nonfiction?

QUESTIONS FOR DEBBIE MACOMBER
**Discuss why you find writing to be such
an apt way to share life lessons. What is
it about writing that seems to help us
chart our lives? Do you think we turn
to literature to find a reflection of ourselves?**

As any writer will tell you, we are primary
storytellers, and it is through story that we
share ourselves and life. Very little in life
happens to me that doesn't somehow, some
way turn up in a book. For me it's how I
process life, how God has wired me. I
believe that stories that resonate most with
us are the ones in which we see ourselves.
When people ask me what I write I generally respond by saying I write popular fiction — slice of life. What gains me readers
is the fact that my slice of life often resembles their own. In *Once Upon a Time,*
you will find several instances in which I
parallel what has happened in my own life
to what took place within a story.

**You begin *Once Upon a Time* with a story
about visiting a library for the first time
as a little girl. Did your early experi-**

ences with books change your life?

God planted a love of story in me from the moment I was handed my first book. Even then He knew what I didn't — that one day I would write books of my own. While I struggled to read, while words and sounds battled within my brain, that day in the library, that first book in my hands that I pressed against my heart, would be a life-altering event for me.

Throughout *Once Upon a Time*, you quote famous writers who have influenced you in some way or whom you admire. If you had to name just one writer as your influence, who would it be and why?

Oh my, you ask the impossible. One name that comes to mind is Catherine Marshall. I devoured her book *Christy.* I have her autograph in my office along with her husband Peter's. But equally compelling is her nonfiction work. Although Catherine and I have never met I would like to consider her a mentor.

What would you name as the major theme(s) of this book? What do you

hope your readers will take away from it?

My objective in writing this book was to help us be aware that we are each writing our own stories, the story of our lives. The choices we make have consequences and often those consequences have far-reaching results. My goal is for us all to live with intention. It's far too easy to drift from one day to the next, putting in our time at work, collecting our paycheck, caught on the treadmill of meritocracy. Our lives are an incredible, wonderful story that needs to be recognized and lived to the fullest.

You urge readers to examine their backstory — the good and the bad, the beautiful and the ugly. Why do you see both positive and negative experiences as worthy of exploration?

The good, the happy unexpected joys in life teach us gratitude. It makes us want to toss our arms in the air and shout, "Thank you, God." But there are parts of our lives that we would all rather leave buried and hidden from view, properly concealed. They too have their lessons. Life is filled with consequences, learning lessons — and often the more painful the lesson, the more profound the lesson . . . if we learn from it.

Describe your morning ritual of reading the Bible. Do you read in any particular order? Do you sit down to write before or after your Bible-reading exercise?

I've read the Bible from beginning to end for more years than I can count now, following Bruce Wilkinson's Walk Thru the Bible reading program, which starts in Genesis and ends with Revelation. What I enjoy about his approach is that every seven to ten days there's a day to reflect on what I've been reading.

For the last three years I've been choosing one grandchild and making notes to him or her along the margins of that Bible and praying for that child every day. It's filled with what I feel God is sharing with me that particular day. At the end of each of the sixty-six books, I write the grandchild I've chosen for that year an extended note. Then on December 31, I give that grandchild the Bible that I have been working on all year.

I do my journal writing, write out my prayers, and fill in my gratitude journal after my Bible reading.

In Chapter 11 you talk about the importance of mentors in the story of our lives. You mention in particular your aunt Betty Stierwalt as a "wise woman" (165) in your life. As a female writer, is it important to you to consider the women in your life who have been of particular influence?

We all have mentors. What's important is that we recognize who they are, thank God for them, and give them the honor and respect that is their due. Over the course of my life and really for all of us, God has brought special people who guide, counsel, and instruct us.

ABOUT THE AUTHOR

Debbie Macomber is one of today's leading voices in women's fiction. A regular on every major bestseller list with more than 140 million copies of her books in print, Debbie's popularity is worldwide, with her books translated into twenty-three languages. Debbie and her husband, Wayne, are the proud parents of four children and grandparents of eight grandchildren. They live in Washington State and winter in Florida.